Roni Rosenthal

102 (One O Two) – Hebrew Online for You

102 fun activities for teaching Hebrew online

A Special Edition for Hebrew/Jewish School Teachers

102 (One O Two) – Online Hebrew for You
102 Fun Activities for *Teaching* Hebrew Online

A Special Edition for Hebrew/Jewish School Teachers
Copyright © 2020 Roni Rosenthal
All rights reserved

Published by The Pencil Pro, StoryTime World
Email: info@101Hebrew.com
Web: 101Hebrew.com

Printed in the United States of America.

No part of this book, including interior design, cover design, and graphics, may be reproduced or transmitted in any form, by any means (electronic, photocopying, recording, or otherwise) without the prior written permission of the publisher.

Library of Congress Control Number: 2020912694   ISBN: 978-0-9792800-6-1

StoryTime World - publishing house

Table of contents

Introduction	7
How To Use This Book	9
Acknowledgments	10
Game No. 1 Show Me the Aleph!	13
Game No. 2 Yoga Pose the Letters	14
Game No. 3 Hang Man	15
Game No. 4 Beginning Sounds	16
Game No. 5 The Wave	17
Game No. 6 Is It in the House?	18
Game No. 7 My Name is … And I am a …	19
Game No. 8 The Color Game	21
Game No. 9 Can you Please Bring? — The Shapes Game	23
Game No. 10 Directions	25
Game No. 11 Yam/Yabasha	26
Game No. 12 It's My Face/Body	27
Game No. 13 Yes/No/Black/White	29
Game No. 14 Who Made That Sound?	30
Game No. 15 We're Going on a Field Trip and We Bring the Aleph-Bet	31
Game No. 16 What's Missing?	32
Game No. 17 What's the Password?	33
Game No. 18 Let's Count – Days of the Week / The Hebrew Calendar	34
Game No. 19 Thumb Up or Down	36
Game No. 20 Telephone in the Chat Box	37
Game No. 21 From a Single Word to a Whole New story	38
Game No. 22 Make it a Category	39
Game No. 23 Opposites	40
Game No. 24 Rhyme it for Me Please	42
Game No. 25 Yes/No Flags	44
Game No. 26 It's One Big Word	45
Game No. 27 Can You Unscramble It?	46
Game No. 28 From Random Letters to Real Words	47

Game No. 29 I Spy 48
Game No. 30 "Go Fetch!" 49
Game No. 31 I Like I Hate 50
Game No. 32 Show and Tell 51
Game No. 33 Pictionary 52
Game No. 34 Dad Went to the Shuk 53
Game No. 35 What's in the Box? 54
Game No. 36 Who am I? 55
Game No. 37 Just Act It Out 56
Game No. 38 Fruit Salad 57
Game No. 39 I'm Sending You a Red Ball. What Can You Send? 58
Game No. 40 Pet Parade 59
Game No. 41 5-Second Rule 60
Game No. 42 No Smiling Now 61
Game No. 43 Blind Bingo 62
Game No. 44 Musical Chairs 63
Game No. 45 Repeat After Me 64
Game No. 46 Anyone for Spelling? 65
Game No. 47 Taboo Words 67
Game No. 48 It's Trivia Time 68
Game No. 49 The Rush for Wiki 69
Game No. 50 Can Google Translate it? 70
Game No. 51 The Last Word 71
Game No. 52 Would you rather … ? 72
Game No. 53 Never Have I Ever … 73
Game No. 54 A Surprise Riddle 75
Game No. 55 Take a Poll 78
Game No. 56 Annotation for All 79
Game No. 57 Say It in Words 80
Game No. 58 The Five Senses 82
Game No. 59 Fortunately, or Unfortunately 83
Game No. 60 This is the Voice … 84
Game No. 61 Are you smarter than …? 85
Game No. 62 There are 50 ways to … Part 1 86

Game No. 63 There are 50 ways to … Part 2	87
Game No. 64 Not your typical Mafia man	89
Game No. 65 Walking on Google Maps	90
Game No. 66 You've Got Mail!	91
Game No. 67 The Echo	92
Game No. 68 A Random Word	93
Game No. 69 Animal or Object?	94
Game No. 70 It's One Long Story After All	95
Game No. 71 What's Your Word?	96
Game No. 72 The Funniest Joke	97
Game No. 73 Advertise it	98
Game No. 74 True or Not?	99
Game No. 75 What Else Can We Make?	100
Game No. 76 What's My Role?	101
Game No. 77 A Quick Draw	102
Game No. 78 What's Wrong?	103
Game No. 79 Describe it for me, please	104
Game No. 80 I'm the Expert!	105
Game No. 81 What Happens Next	106
Game No. 82 But … Why?	107
Game No. 83 How do you Make … ?	109
Game No. 84 Are You Ready for Math?	110
Game No. 85 Are You Ready for Math? Word Riddles	112
Game No. 86 Are You Ready for Math? Gematria	113
Game No. 87 Who is He and How Old is He Now?	115
Game No. 88 Order in Court	116
Game No. 89 Follow my Instructions	117
Game No. 90 Book Party!	119
Game No. 91 Interview Me, Please	120
Game No. 92 My Hidden Secret	121
Game No. 93 Read My lips	122
Game No. 94 Where is He?	123
Game No. 95 What Are You Selling?	124
Game No. 96 Why are You Late?	125

Game No. 97 Domino of Words 126
Game No. 98 **What's for Dinner?** 127
Game No. 99 Make Flashcards Facts 128
Game No. 100 More Math in Hebrew 129
Game No. 101 What's in the Dish? 130
Game No. 102 Lip-Sync Battles 131
Addendum 132

Introduction

- **Are** you teaching Hebrew classes **online**?
- **Do** you feel that sometimes your students are drifting off?
- **Are** you looking for more ways to engage your students in the lesson?
- **Are** you looking for other ways to support the learning?
- **Are** you tired of asking your students at the end of class to tell you two new things they have learned today?
- **Are** you looking for Hebrew refreshers for the beginning, end, or middle of the lesson?
- **How** about introductory games at the beginning of the year?
- **How** about teaching new vocabulary through games?
- **How** about practicing Hebrew grammar, reading, writing and conversational skills through games?
- **How** about just having fun in Hebrew?

Learning through play, also known as game-based learning, is a well-known educational method that is effective for transferring content, information or knowledge to make sense in the student world.

Making learning fun and actively engaging students in the lessons help students pay attention and stay focused. Games can create a dynamic that inspires students to develop skills and capabilities as they focus on the activities of the game.

Shalom, my name is Dr. Roni Rosenthal and for the past 10 years I've served as a Hebrew school Education Director in Washington D.C. area. I'm also a Hebrew professor and the Director of Judaic Studies at The University of Maryland, Baltimore County.

I've been teaching Online Hebrew classes (as well as Hybrid courses and other Jewish Studies courses) since 2013. I work with students at various Hebrew levels, from beginners to advanced, and in various capacities.

Over the years, I have used different instructional Video-conferencing technology platforms, such as Zoom, WebEx, Canvas, Blackboard, Go2Meetings and others, and have taught synchronous and asynchronous courses.

I have collected over 1,000 (!) games to practice Hebrew online.

In this book I share with you the ones I graded as "my top list."

The games in this book were the most popular, captured the interest of my students, and engaged them in the lesson. Above all, through the use of these games, I was able to teach my students something new, whether it was new vocabulary words or reinforcement of basic sentences, and to witness the students grow more confident with conversational Hebrew skills.

Although I'm not tech-savvy, I found it easy to use tools like Videos, Chat-Box, Annotations and Breakout rooms. The activities suggested in this book are based on those basic tools.

I started working with kids as a scout's guide when I was 16 years old. Even now, after many years of teaching in formal and non-formal structures, in Hebrew schools, Jewish Day schools and at the University, I strongly believe in the advantages of teaching through games.

Using games during the lessons not only motivates students to learn more, but also gives them the confidence of using the language, creates emotional connection and dedication to learning and provides opportunities for immediate feedback and extra practice. The games can be customized to any topic or a specific unit.

While playing the games, students collaborate, communicate, and interact in a second language without challenges as the game excitement and the goal of winning points overtakes any barriers.

In 2009, I published my book **"101 Let's Have Fun** – 101 Fun Activities that Reinforce Learning in the Hebrew Language." The book became successful immediately and was placed as a Best-Seller in this category.

In this book, **"102 Hebrew Online for You,"** I present 102 games and activities to reinforce learning the Hebrew language Online.

No matter the Hebrew level of the students or their ages, learners will always enjoy a few minutes of a refresher.

Use the activities suggested in this book for a successful, fun and engaging lesson. And have fun!

How To Use This Book

Most of the games presented in this book do not need any prior preparation (and if they do, it's minimal). Most of the games do not require the use of any special materials, other than basic things you can find on Google images or YouTube clips.

The games in this book are divided by Hebrew levels — beginner, intermediate, and advanced. Use this simply as a guide; there are no hard and fast rules. Teachers are the best judges of whether a game is suitable for their classes. If you think your students will enjoy it, go for it!

Acknowledgments

I would like to thank my colleagues and students for the hours spent wisely and fruitfully trying out my Hebrew games and providing their feedback.

I would like to thank my family, my mom, my sister and my children, Shachar and Kiki. A special thanks to Kobi, Shoko and Krembo. Thank you all for your support, help, brainstorming, and patience. Thank you for being my audience.

So grab the book and let's play ...

Enjoy.

Tips for having a successful Online Lesson

1. Log into your session a few minutes early to ensure a proper technical connection.

2. In advance of your session, make sure your camera, microphone, and audio work well and that all options are applicable (screen share, annotations, etc.). It's highly recommended to schedule a practice meeting in advance to practice using screen sharing, Annotations, chat box, breakout rooms, etc.

3. It is highly recommended to record the session for safety reasons.

4. **It's recommended that students log in from their** kitchens, offices or living rooms.

5. Before playing a game, make sure to be very clear about the instructions. If needed, complete a practice round.

6. **Games should be played in a safe and comfortable environment.** If there's any safety issue at risk, do not play the game.

7. Each one of the games can be used as a model. Adjust the game to your needs.

8. Don't let the game take over the lesson.

9. Always be positive. Even when students do not win games, don't let them get frustrated. Encourage them by saying something like, "You did great. I'm not so sure I could have done it any better ..."

10. Don't let the game go on for too long.

11. Be creative and remember to enjoy the game yourself.

Games for Beginners to Intermediate Hebrew Levels

Game No. 1
Show Me the Aleph!

Learning Objectives: To practice the Hebrew letters
Suitable for Hebrew Levels: Beginners
Playing Time: 10 minutes
Materials/Resources Needed: Students should have various materials they can use to form the letter as markers, empty toilet paper rolls, glue sticks, books, etc.

Helpful Hints: This is a great game to practice the Hebrew letters while being creative.

How to play:

Via the chat box, privately assign each student a letter from the Aleph-Bet.

Each student then has two minutes to create and present the letter they received using materials they can find in the house.

Examples of materials include markers to form the letter, empty toilet paper rolls, glue sticks, books, etc.

Students should monitor the chat box while thinking how to create their letters.

When finished, each student presents the letter in the video.

Game No. 2
Yoga Pose the Letters

Learning Objectives: To practice decoding and Hebrew letters
Suitable for Hebrew Levels: Beginners
Playing Time: 10 minutes
Materials/Resources Needed: None

Helpful Hints: This game is a fun way to get students moving while learning their Aleph-Bet letters. It's a fun way to work on gross motor skills while learning.

How to play:

Ask students to stand up and move away from their chairs.

Via the chat box, privately assign each student a letter from the Aleph-Bet.

Ask the students to pose in the shape of their letters using their fingers, hands or bodies and being as creative as possible.

To challenge students, ask them not to repeat the same hand motion or pose that another student has already used.

The rest of the students need to guess what letter the pose represents.
Students may use script or print Hebrew letters.

Game No. 3
Hang Man

> **Learning Objectives:** Practice Hebrew letters, spelling and decoding
> **Suitable for Hebrew Levels:** Beginners
> **Playing Time:** 10 minutes
> **Materials/Resources Needed:** None

Helpful Hints: This game works well to review letters or teach new phrases.

How to play:
Ask students to come up with a word or a phrase they have recently learned and send it to you privately in the chat box.
The teacher writes one dash on the whiteboard for each letter of the word or words chosen, and shares the screen. Do not forget to leave a space between words.

Students should guess one letter at a time until they find the right word(s).
The teacher should fill in the letter (everywhere it appears) on the dash or dashes each time a person guesses correctly.
Start drawing a hangman and add a line when students do not guess correctly. Begin by drawing a head attached to the short vertical line. You can add eyes, ears, nose, hair, body, legs, arms, etc. If the drawing is completed before the students guess the correct word, then they lose a point. If they guess the word before the picture is complete, then they win a point.

Game No. 4
Beginning Sounds

> **Learning Objectives:** Decoding letters and vowels in Hebrew/ listening comprehension
> **Suitable for Hebrew Levels:** Beginners
> **Playing Time:** 5-10 minutes
> **Materials/Resources Needed:** None / You could use flashcards or write the letters and vowels on a whiteboard/paper.
> **Variations:** Combine words or instructions.

Helpful Tips: This game works well at the beginning of the year and for basic decoding.

How to play:
The teacher instructs the students that whenever they hear the combination of a specific letter and vowel — for example: בָּ = The letter Bet with Kamatz or Patach (makes the sounds of Ba') — they need to put their hands on their heads or jump up and down in the chair.

The teacher then reads a short text in Hebrew. Students must listen carefully and follow the instructions given.

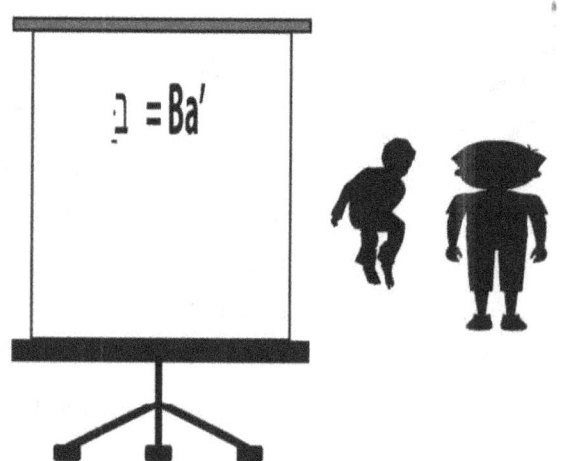

Variations: Teachers may choose to give more than one instruction or complete words. For example: When you hear the word גָמָל you must stand up, but when you hear the word אֹהֶל you must sit down quickly.

Game No. 5
The Wave

Learning Objectives: Practice Hebrew letters
Suitable for Hebrew Levels: Beginners
Playing Time: 3-5 minutes
Materials/Resources Needed: None

Helpful Hints: This game is a fun way to practice the Hebrew Aleph-Bet. You can go from Aleph to Tav and then back from Tav to Aleph.

א ב ג ד ה

How to play:
Are you familiar with the Wave at sport events, when people stand up briefly, yell, raise their arms and then immediately sit down? Yes? This game uses the same concept but with letters.

Prior to playing the game, the teacher assigns each student a letter from the Aleph Bet. The list may be distributed in advance or via the chat box.

During an agreed signal, the teacher asks the first student with the letter Aleph to stand up for a second, raise both hands and yell "Aleph." As soon as the first student sits down, the student who has the letter Bet should do the same: stand up, raise both hands, yell "Bet," and sit down. The game goes until the last student yells "Tav."

The teacher may ask students either to repeat from Aleph or start with the last letter, Tav, and go back until the first student yells "Aleph."

Game No. 6
Is It in the House?

> **Learning Objectives:** Practice Hebrew letters and vocabulary words in Hebrew
> **Suitable for Hebrew Levels:** Beginners to Intermediate
> **Playing Time:** 5-10 minutes
> **Materials/Resources Needed:** None
> **Variations:** Challenge the students by not allowing them to repeat an item more than once. Allow students to use Google to find pictures as their answers.

Helpful Tips: Make sure to be very clear about the rules prior to playing the game.
This game works well as a practice after teaching the vocabulary words or as a refresher.

How to play:
The teacher calls out a name of a letter in Hebrew, for example: Gimmel. The students have one minute (or longer) to get an object in the house that begins with the letter Gimmel.

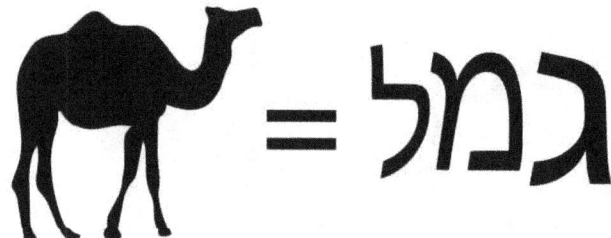

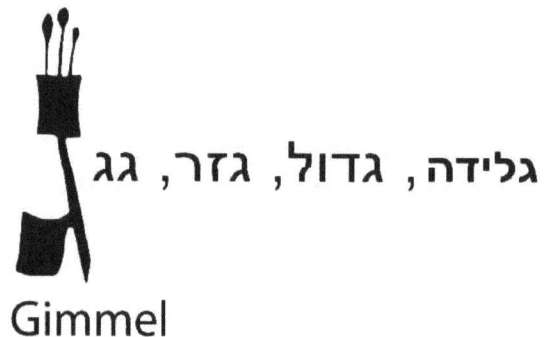

Gimmel

Variations: Teachers may decide to add more challenges like: The item's name must start with the letter Gimmel and end with the letter Lamed. The students can quickly Google and upload a picture of גָּמָל = Camel.

Game No. 7
My Name is ... And I am a ...

Learning Objectives: Practice Hebrew vocabulary
Suitable for Hebrew Levels: Beginners
Playing Time: 5-10 minutes
Materials/Resources Needed: None
Variations: Students repeat the previous name and object, and then add their own name and object.

Helpful Hints: You can take a couple of turns playing this game. Just ask the students to choose a different item, animal, or object each time. This game can be played at the beginning of the year or as an ice breaker.

How to play:
Teachers begin by saying their names and an object that starts with the first letter of that name. Each student says his/her name and adds the name of an object that starts with the first letter of his/her name. For example: My name is

Roni and I am רַכֶּבֶת (a train).
Older students may also try to explain the connection between their names and the object. For example: I'm רַכֶּבֶת, because I'm always in a hurry.

Variations: Students, in their turns, repeat the previous name and object, and then add their own names and objects. For example: He is Moshe מַיִם (water), and I am David דָג (fish).

LETTERS AND WORDS   אוֹת וּמִלָּה

א	אֲבַטִּיחַ, אוֹטוֹבּוּס, אַמְבַּטְיָה, אָרוֹן, אַרְמוֹן
ב	בַּיִת, בְּגָדִים, בֻּבָּה, בַּנְק, בַּקְבּוּק
ג	גְּבִינָה, גִּיטָרָה, גִּנָּה, גַּלְגַּל, גְּלִידָה
ד	דָּג, דֶּגֶל, דִּירָה, דֶּלֶת, דֶּשֶׁא
ה	הַגָּדָה, הוֹדָעָה, הַפְתָּעָה, הַצָּגָה, הַר
ו	וִילָה, וִילוֹן, וָפֶל, וֶרֶד, וָרֹד
ז	זְבוּב, זָהָב, זַיִת, זְכוּכִית, זַמָּר
ח	חֲבִילָה, חֶבֶל, חָבֵר, חַג, חֶדֶר
ט	טַבְלָה, טַבַּעַת, טְחִינָה, טִיּוּל, טֶלֶוִיזְיָה
י	יוֹם, יוֹנָה, יֶלֶד, יָם, יַעַר
כ	כְּבִישׁ, כַּדּוּר, כּוֹכָב, כֻּרְסָא, כִּנּוֹר
ל	לוּחַ, לֶחֶם, לַחְמָנִיָּה, לִימוֹן, לֵיצָן
מ	מִבְחָן, מִגְדָּל, מִדְבָּר, מְדוּרָה, מוֹנִית
נ	נָמֵל, נָמֵר, נַעַל, נֵרוֹת, נְשִׁיקָה
ס	סְטוּדֶנְט, סִירָה, סָלָט, סֵפֶר, סִפְרִיָּה
ע	עַגְבָנִיָּה, עוּגָה, עִתּוֹן, עֵץ, עָנָן
פ	פִּטְרִיָּה, פִּיצָה, פִּתָּה, פְּסַנְתֵּר, פְּרִי
צ	צָב, צִיּוּר, צִפּוֹר, צַלַּחַת, צְפַרְדֵּעַ
ק	קוֹלְנוֹעַ, קֻפְסָה, קוֹף, קוֹץ, קְעָרָה
ר	רֹאשׁ, רֶגֶל, רָהִיטִים, רְחוֹב, רַכֶּבֶת
ש	שׁוֹטֵר, שֻׁלְחָן, שׁוֹקוֹלָד, שָׁטִיחַ, שֶׁמֶשׁ
ת	תַּחֲנָה, תִּינוֹק, תִּיק, תְּמוּנָה, תְּעוּדָה

Game No. 8
The Color Game

> **Learning Objectives:** Practice the names of the colors in Hebrew
> **Suitable for Hebrew Levels:** Beginners to Intermediate
> **Playing Time:** 5-10 minutes
> **Materials/Resources Needed:** None
> **Variations:** Use main colors for beginner level and advanced colors for intermediate level.

Helpful Tips: Make sure to be very clear about the rules prior to playing the game. This game works well as a practice after teaching the colors or as a refresher.

How to play:
The teacher calls out a name of a color in Hebrew or presents a color flashcard or an image on screen: For example: צָהֹב (Yellow).
The students have one minute (or longer) to get any object in the house in that color.

אָדוֹם = Yellow
צָהֹב = Red

Variations: Teachers may decide on a different time for each color (as it might be more challenging to find items in the house that are purple, for example), or how many items to bring in this color. For example: "Bring five things into the house that are אָדֹם (Red), or the first to bring a כָּחֹל (blue) item wins points.

A safety tip: Add a condition that students must bring the items back without letting any other item fall.

THE NAMES OF THE COLORS — שְׁמוֹת הַצְּבָעִים

Color	צֶבַע
Red	אָדוֹם
Grey	אָפוֹר
Maroon	בּוֹרְדּוֹ
Pink	וָרוֹד
Gold	זָהָב
Khaki	חָאקִי
Brown	חוּם
Turquoise	טוּרְקִיז
Green	יָרוֹק
Olive-Green	יָרוֹק זַיִת
Blue	כָּחוֹל
Silver	כֶּסֶף
Orange	כָּתוֹם
White	לָבָן
Purple	סָגֹל
Yellow	צָהוֹב
Black	שָׁחוֹר
Light Blue	תְּכֵלֶת

Game No. 9
Can you Please Bring? — The Shapes Game

> **Learning Objectives:** Practice the names of shapes in Hebrew
> **Suitable for Hebrew Levels:** Beginners to Intermediate
> **Playing Time:** 5-10 minutes
> **Materials/Resources Needed:** Virtual images on screen or flashcards with shapes
> **Variations:** Use main shapes for beginner level and advanced shapes for intermediate level.

Helpful Tips: Make sure to be very clear about the rules prior to playing the game. This game works well as a practice after teaching the shapes or as a refresher.

How to play:
The teacher calls out a name of a shape in Hebrew or presents a shape flashcard or an image on the screen: For example: מְשֻׁלָּשׁ (triangle). The students run to get an object in the shape that was called.

Variation: A nice variation is to combine colors and shapes. For example, the teacher may call: "Bring an item that is מְשֻׁלָּשׁ כָּחֹל (a blue triangle), or a רִבּוּעַ אָדֹם (a red square), etc."

A safety tip: Students must bring the items back without making another item fall.

שְׁמוֹת הַצּוּרוֹת בְּעִבְרִית וּבָאַנְגְּלִית
THE NAME OF THE SHAPES IN HEBREW AND ENGLISH

English	Hebrew
Oval	אֶלִיפְּסָה
Trapezium	טְרָפֵז
Star	כּוֹכָב
Heart	לֵב
Pentagon	מְחֻמָּשׁ
Rectangle	מַלְבֵּן
Diamond	מְעֻיָּן
Triangle	מְשֻׁלָּשׁ
Hexagon	מְשֻׁשֶּׁה
Octagon	מְתֻמָּן
Circle	עָגוּל
Square	רִבּוּעַ

3D SHAPES
צוּרוֹת בִּתְלַת מֵמַד

Cylinder	גָּלִיל
Cone	קוֹנוּס
Cube	קֻבִּיָּה
Pyramid	פִּירָמִידָה
Sphere	כַּדּוּר
Prism	מִנְסָרָה (פְּרִיזְמָה)

Game No. 10
Directions

> **Learning Objectives:** Learn and practice directions (left, right, up, down) in Hebrew
> **Suitable for Hebrew Levels:** Beginners to Intermediate
> **Playing Time:** 5-10 minutes
> **Materials/Resources Needed:** None
> **Variations:** Start with basic directions (left, right, up, down) for beginners. Add advanced (forward, back, turn around, or combine directions with body parts, like hands up, head down, etc.) for intermediate level.

Helpful Tips: This is a fun game requiring students to move around.

How to play:
Ask the students to stand up and move away from their chairs.

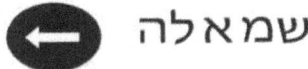

The teacher demonstrates first and students follow.
The teacher calls: קָדִימָה (forward); everybody takes one step forward.
The teacher calls: אֲחוֹרָה (back); everybody takes one step back.
The teacher calls: יָמִינָה (right); everybody takes one step to the right.
The teacher calls: שְׂמֹאלָה (left); everybody takes one step to the left.
The teacher calls: לְמַעְלָה (up); everybody looks up.
The teacher calls: לְמַטָה (down); everybody looks down.
Every now and then, the teacher should repeat the same instruction twice or try to get the students confused. Once students get confused, they leave the game and sit back down or just leave for two minutes and come back.
A safety tip: Students must have enough space to move around, so they don't bump into an object in their areas.

Game No. 11
Yam/Yabasha

> **Learning Objectives:** Practice Hebrew vocabulary
> **Suitable for Hebrew Levels:** Beginners to Intermediate
> **Playing Time:** 10-15 minutes
> **Materials/Resources Needed:** None / You could use flashcards or write the words on a whiteboard/paper.
> **Variations:** Use with any opposite words.

Helpful Tips: This is a fun game requiring students to move around.

How to play:
Ask students to stand up and move away from their chairs.
When the teacher calls: יָם (ocean/sea), students should jump one step forward and pretend to swim. When the teacher calls: יַבָּשָׁה (land), students should jump back to their starting points.

Variations: The teacher may change and use **any opposite** words. For example, when the teacher says: גָּבוֹהַּ (tall), students jump forward. With נָמוּךְ (short), they jump back.

Another variation for intermediate or advanced levels: Once the teacher calls out singular form words, students jump back, and for plural form words students jump forward. (The same concept can be used for masculine/feminine nouns.)

A safety tip: Students must have enough space to move around, so they don't bump into an object in their areas.

Game No. 12
It's My Face/Body

> **Learning Objectives:** Practice face/body parts in Hebrew
> **Suitable for Hebrew Levels:** Beginners to Intermediate
> **Playing Time:** 10-15 minutes
> **Materials/Resources Needed:** None / You could use flashcards or write the words on the white board/paper.
> **Variations:** Use basic body parts for beginners and more complex face/body parts for intermediate and advanced levels. Use a combination of body parts, adjectives or color. For example: She has long brown hair, or his big blue eyes are pretty, etc.

Helpful Tips: This game works well as a beginning-of-the-class review or after introducing the face/body parts first.

How to play:
This game is based on the same principle as the game "Simon says."
The teacher calls out or points to a face or a body part. Students touch the corresponding face or body part on their own bodies, but only when the teacher says, "Simon says." If the teacher calls out or points to a body part and does not say, "Simon says," the students should not follow the instruction. The teacher may add: "right hand on the left side of your head" or "left foot on the right knee," etc.
This game gets really funny when the teacher tries to get the students confused by touching an ear and saying, "Simon says touch your nose."
For advanced levels, the teacher may share pictures of famous people and ask students to describe their physical appearances.

יד ימין על רגל שמאל   יד שמאל על הגב

BODY PARTS IN HEBREW   אֶבְרֵי הַגּוּף בְּעִבְרִית

Head	רֹאשׁ
Face	פָּנִים
Neck	צַוָּאר
Shoulder	כָּתֵף
Chest	חָזֶה
Arm	זְרוֹעַ
Elbow	מַרְפֵּק
Hand	יָד
Belly	בֶּטֶן
Waist	מֹתֶן
Leg	רֶגֶל
Knee	בֶּרֶךְ
Foot	כַּף רֶגֶל
Fingers	אֶצְבָּעוֹת
Thigh	יָרֵךְ
Ankle	קַרְסֹל
Calf	שׁוֹק
Palm	כַּף יָד
Heel	עָקֵב
Back	גַּב

Game No. 13
Yes/No/Black/White

> **Learning Objectives:** Practice conversational Hebrew
> **Suitable for Hebrew Levels:** Beginners to Intermediate
> **Playing Time:** 10-15 minutes
> **Materials/Resources Needed:** None / You could use flashcards or write the words on a whiteboard/paper.
> **Variations:** Use visual images/flashcards or have volunteers ask questions.

Helpful Tips: This game is similar to the "Taboo words" game, but this time the taboo words are constant (do not change with each object). This is a very popular game in Israel.

How to play:
There are two options for playing this game:

Option 1: The teacher presents a visual image (or a flashcard) of an object. Ask a student to describe this object to the class without using the "Taboo" words. For example, "Please describe everything you know about חָלָב (milk)." The taboo words for this game are: כֵּן (Yes), לֹא (No), שָׁחוֹר (Black), לָבָן (White).

Option 2: The teacher or a "volunteer" asks each student a question in turn. Each student answers the question without using the "Taboo" words: כֵּן (Yes), לֹא (No), שָׁחוֹר (Black), לָבָן (White).

Questions may be, for example: "Is today Friday?"

If you are not using flashcards, you may simply write the taboo words on the whiteboard and share your screen with the group.

Game No. 14
Who Made That Sound?

> **Learning Objectives:** Practice the names of the animals in Hebrew
> **Suitable for Hebrew Levels:** Beginners to Intermediate
> **Playing Time:** 10-15 minutes
> **Materials/Resources Needed:** YouTube/animal sounds on your phone

Helpful Hints: This is a fun activity. Make sure to teach the names of the animals first.

How to Play: The teacher plays YouTube clips or phone ringtones with sounds of various animals, without presenting the image of the animal.

Hav-Hav = כלב = 🐕

Students need to guess the name of the animal (in Hebrew) that makes this sound. Remember — in Hebrew a duck goes Ga-Ga, a dog goes Hav-Hav, and a rooster goes Ku-Ku-Ri-Ku-Ku.

Ga-Ga = ברווז = 🦆

Game No. 15
We're Going on a Field Trip and We Bring the Aleph-Bet

Learning Objectives: Practice Hebrew vocabulary
Suitable for Hebrew Levels: Beginners
Playing Time: 5-10 minutes
Materials/Resources Needed: None
Variations: Students may be asked to repeat previous responses.

Helpful Hints: This is a fun game to practice Hebrew vocabulary.

How to play:
The teacher starts by saying: "We're going on a field trip and we bring …"
אֲנַחְנוּ הוֹלְכִים לְטִיּוּל וְלוֹקְחִים
The first student needs to say something that begins with the letter Aleph.
The next student needs to say something that begins with the letter Bet and so on, until the letter Tav.

Variations: The second student may repeat the first item that had been said, starting with the letter Aleph, and adds one item that starts with the letter Bet. The third student repeats the previous items and adds an item with the letter Gimel and so on.

Game No. 16
What's Missing?

> **Learning Objectives:** Practice Hebrew vocabulary
> **Suitable for Hebrew Levels:** Beginners to Intermediate
> **Playing Time:** 10 minutes
> **Materials/Resources Needed:** Use real items, visual images or write the words on a whiteboard/paper.

Helpful Tips: A great game to review vocabulary and practice memory skills.

How to play:
The teacher presents a few images, words or visual photos of different items. It's highly recommended to use at least 10 to 15 different objects, but not more than 20.
First, the teacher should review the names of the items or objects presented.

Students have just one minute to look at the images and memorize them. Then, students close their eyes and the teacher pulls away one card. Students need to guess which card or object is missing.
Items can be different fruits/vegetables, Jewish holidays/symbols, or random items.
Teachers may want to play this game by sharing virtual images through their screens or with magnets and a cookie sheet.

Game No. 17
What's the Password?

> **Learning Objectives:** Review Hebrew vocabulary
> **Suitable for Hebrew Levels:** Beginners to Intermediate
> **Playing Time:** 5 minutes
> **Materials/Resources Needed:** None
> **Variations:** The "Password" can be a word or a phrase from a specific given vocabulary list.

Helpful Tips: This game works well as a review of a specific vocabulary list or a specific theme. This game is best to use in the middle of the lesson or as a quick review at the end of class.

How to play:
In order to move on to the next topic or to conclude the lesson, the teacher asks: "What's the password?" Each student has one chance to guess (from a specific given vocabulary list) what the "password" may possibly be.

The teacher should decide on a specific word (or a phrase) in advance.

If none of the students guess the correct "password," the teacher may want to give a hint.

A specific list of vocabulary must be used for this game. A vocabulary word or phrase can be, for example: One new word/phrase from today's lesson, a word that belongs to a specific category, or a polite phrase like: תּוֹדָה וּלְהִתְרָאוֹת (Thank you and see you later).

Game No. 18
Let's Count – Days of the Week / The Hebrew Calendar

Learning Objectives: Practice the days of the week or counting the Hebrew calendar
Suitable for Hebrew Levels: Beginners
Playing Time: 5-10 minutes
Materials/Resources Needed: None
Variations: Begin to count with a different day/month or count back from Saturday (the last day of the week) or Elul (the last month of the Jewish year).

Helpful Hints: This game should be played a couple of times during the year. Use the variations suggested above to make the game more fun.

How to play:
The teacher explains and demonstrates the principle of counting the days of the week in Hebrew or the Hebrew calendar.

The teacher starts by saying יוֹם רִאשׁוֹן (Sunday). Then, the teacher decides who is next to "steal the spotlight." The next student should say יוֹם שֵׁנִי (Monday) and so on.

When playing the Hebrew calendar game, the teacher should start with תִּשְׁרֵי (the first month), and the next student continues with חֶשְׁוָן and so on.

Variations: The teacher says: If הַיוֹם (today) is יוֹם שְׁלִישִׁי then מָחָר (tomorrow) is ... and אֶתְמוֹל (yesterday) was ...

DAYS OF THE WEEK IN HEBREW   יְמֵי הַשָׁבוּעַ בְּעִבְרִית

יוֹם רִאשׁוֹן	Sunday
יוֹם שֵׁנִי	Monday
יוֹם שְׁלִישִׁי	Tuesday
יוֹם רְבִיעִי	Wednesday
יוֹם חֲמִישִׁי	Thursday
יוֹם שִׁשִׁי	Friday
יוֹם שַׁבָּת	Saturday
הַיּוֹם	Today
מָחָר	Tomorrow
אֶתְמוֹל	Yesterday
שִׁלְשׁוֹם	The day before yesterday
מָחֳרָתַיִם	The day after tomorrow
שָׁבוּעַ	A week
שְׁבוּעַיִם	Two weeks
שָׁנָה	A year
שְׁנָתַיִם	Two years
חֹדֶשׁ	A month
חוֹדְשַׁיִם	Two months

Game No. 19
Thumb Up or Down

> **Learning Objectives:** To practice listening comprehension skills in Hebrew
> **Suitable for Hebrew Levels:** Beginners
> **Playing Time:** 10 minutes
> **Materials/Resources Needed:** A book or a short story in Hebrew
> **Variations:** Questions may include feedback questions.

Helpful Hints: This game works well with beginners who have basic Hebrew vocabulary.

How to play:

The teacher starts reading a book in Hebrew. Every now and then, the teacher stops and asks a follow-up question to which the answer can only be a yes or no.

If students answer yes, they raise their thumbs up and if the answer is no, they put their thumbs down.

Questions may include feedback questions, such as, "Do you like the story so far?" or "Did you understand at least 50% of what I read so far?" Other questions may be based on the story content. For example: If the boy just ate 10 apples, put your thumb up. If it's a different number, put your thumb down.

כן

לא

Game No. 20
Telephone in the Chat Box

Learning Objectives: Practice Hebrew vocabulary
Suitable for Hebrew Levels: Beginners
Playing Time: 5-10 minutes
Materials/Resources Needed: None

Helpful Hints: This game gets very funny.
The teacher must instruct the students not to copy and paste the word or phrase, but to retype it in the chat box. <u>Students should have access to a virtual Hebrew Keyboard</u>.

How to play:
The teacher sends a word, a sentence or a phrase privately via the chat box to one of the students. The first student who receives the word or phrase sends it to the next student via the chat box, and so on. Each student transfers the word, sentence, or phrase to the next student in class via the chat box until it returns to the teacher.

The teacher compares the word that was received from the last student with the original word.

Game No. 21
From a Single Word to a Whole New story

Learning Objectives: Practice Hebrew vocabulary
Suitable for Hebrew Levels: Beginners
Playing Time: 5-10 minutes
Materials/Resources Needed: None

Helpful Hints: This game gets very funny.

How to play:

The teacher sends one single word or one beginning sentence privately via the chat box to one of the students. The first student who receives the word or sentence adds another sentence and then copies both sentences and sends them both to the next student in line via the chat box. The third student adds another sentence and then copies all three sentences and sends them via chat box to the next student in line, and so on. Each student must add a sentence to create one big story.

Once the full story is received from the last student, the teacher reads it out loud to the group.

Game No. 22
Make it a Category

> **Learning Objectives:** Practice basic Hebrew vocabulary
> **Suitable for Hebrew Levels:** Beginners
> **Playing Time:** 5-10 minutes
> **Materials/Resources Needed:** None
> **Variations:** The teacher may assign the category or theme or have the students come up with themes, like transportation, musical instruments, holidays, etc.

Helpful Hints: This is a great way to review basic vocabulary.

How to play:

There are three ways to play this game:

1) The teacher divides the class into three breakout rooms. Each group has one minute to come up with as many words as possible related to this category in Hebrew.
   For example: The teacher calls out: "Israeli Food." Students need to come up with as many words as possible related to Israeli food in Hebrew. The group who has the most category related words wins.

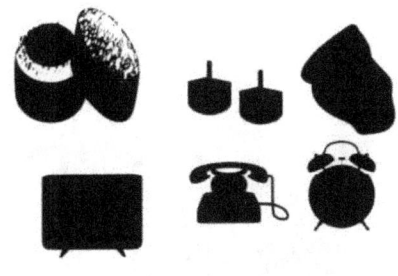

פירות וירקות   ספורט

2) The teacher calls out a theme or a category, for example: "things you may find in a house." The teacher then starts "browsing" between the students' videos until focusing on one student, who must say a word (or a sentence) related to the category. The teacher then moves to the next student. However, students should not repeat something that was already said; therefore, they should prepare in advance their second and/or third option.

3) This game can be played via the chat box. The teacher assigns a category and types it into the chat box. Students must keep an eye on the chat box and type in their word related to that category as soon as possible. If their word was already written by another student, they must come up with another word.

Game No. 23
Opposites

> **Learning Objectives:** Practice Hebrew vocabulary
> **Suitable for Hebrew Levels:** Beginners
> **Playing Time:** 5-10 minutes
> **Materials/Resources Needed:** None
> **Variations:** The teacher can assign the opposite words or let the students come up with opposite words themselves.

Helpful Hints: This is a great way to review basic vocabulary.

How to Play: There are three ways to play this game:

Option 1: The teacher divides the class into two groups: boys vs. girls, by birthdays, last names, or any other way. One group says a word, and the other group needs to come up with the opposite word. Alternate the groups, or use "representatives."

Option 2: The teacher uses the chat box and types in words. The student who comes up first with the opposite word and types it in the chat box correctly wins.

Option 3: The teacher calls out words. Then, the teacher "browses" between the videos and randomly puts the "spotlight" on a student who gets 20 seconds to find the opposite word or the "spotlight" moves on to another student.

A Safety Tip: When using the "spotlight" video option, make sure that students understand in advance that it's Okay if they do not know the answer or make a mistake.

רְשִׁימַת הֲפָכִים בְּעִבְרִית וּבְאַנְגְּלִית
OPPOSITE WORDS IN HEBREW AND ENGLISH

Tall – Short	גָּבוֹהַּ - נָמוּךְ
Day – Night	יוֹם - לַיְלָה
Hot – Cold	חַם - קַר
Close – Far away	קָרוֹב - רָחוֹק
Cheap – Expensive	זוֹל - יָקָר
Poor – Rich	עָנִי - עָשִׁיר
Sick – Healthy	חוֹלֶה - בָּרִיא
Wet – Dry	רָטֹב – יָבֵשׁ
Awake – Sleep	עֵר – יָשֵׁן
First – Last	רִאשׁוֹן - אַחֲרוֹן
Clean – Dirty	נָקִי – מְלֻכְלָךְ
Easy – Hard	קַל - קָשֶׁה
Dark – Clear	כֵּהֶה - בָּהִיר
Sweet – Bitter	מָתוֹק – מַר
Full – Empty	מָלֵא - רֵיק
Outside – Inside	מִחוּץ – בְּתוֹךְ
Complete – Broken	שָׁלֵם – שָׁבוּר
Happy – Sad	שָׂמֵחַ – עָצוּב
Closed – Open	סָגוּר – פָּתוּחַ
Before – After	לִפְנֵי – אַחֲרֵי
Organized – Mess	מְסֻדָּר – מְבֻלְגָּן
Small – Big	קָטָן – גָּדוֹל
Curve – Straight	עָקֹם – יָשָׁר

Game No. 24
Rhyme it for Me Please

> **Learning Objectives:** Practice Hebrew vocabulary
> **Suitable for Hebrew Levels:** Beginners to Intermediate
> **Playing Time:** 5-10 minutes
> **Materials/Resources Needed:** Use children's nursery rhyme books in Hebrew.

Helpful Hints: This game works well once the students possess enough vocabulary, mid to end of the school year.

How to play:
There are two ways to play this game:
1) The basic word search — The teacher calls out a word that needs to be rhymed. The first student who calls out a rhyming word wins a point.

2) The teacher presents a visual image on the screen. The first student to find the first rhyming word wins one point, but the second student to find an additional rhyming word wins two points. The third student to find a third rhyming word of the same visual wins three points.

RHYMING WORDS — מִלִים מִתְחָרְזוֹת

קַר	מַר
סַבָּא	אַבָּא
בָּלוֹן	וִילוֹן
נָחָשׁ	חָדָשׁ
גַּג	דָּג
מָרָק	בָּרָק
שָׁם	קָם
רַעַם	פַּעַם
שָׁטִיחַ	אֲבַטִּיחַ
מָלוּחַ	תַּפּוּחַ
עַכָּבִישׁ	כָּרִישׁ
קִיר	סִיר
כּוֹחַ	מוֹחַ
רוּחַ	לוּחַ
סָלוֹן	חַלּוֹן
גֶּרֶב	עֶרֶב

Game No. 25
Yes/No Flags

> **Learning Objectives:** To practice conversational Hebrew or questions with a "yes" or "no" answer
> **Suitable for Hebrew Levels:** Beginners to Intermediate
> **Playing Time:** 5-10 minutes
> **Materials/Resources Needed:** Flags/ White paper with the words "Yes" and "No." Teachers should prepare review questions in advance.
> **Variations:** Each student holds two flags: One flag says "Yes" and the other "No." Or divide the class into two groups, with one group holding the "Yes" flag and the other group holding the "No" flag.

Helpful Hints: This game is easy to play. Have students make their own flags.

How to play:
Before starting the game, ask students to take two pieces of white paper and write כֵּן (Yes) on one page and לֹא (No) on the other.

Younger students may want to draw pictures of things that they like on the "Yes" page and things they don't like on the "No" page.

For the game: The teacher asks a question. If the answer is : כֵּן, students lift up the "Yes" flag; if the answer is לֹא, students lift the "No" flag. Questions could be things like: "Is שֻׁלְחָן the right word for a chair?" etc.

Variations:
The teacher divides the class into two groups. One group holds the "Yes" flag, and the other holds the "No" flag. Alternatively, instead of using flags, you can just have students stand up if they think the answer is yes, and sit down if they think the answer is no.

Game No. 26
It's One Big Word

> **Learning Objectives:** Practice Hebrew vocabulary
> **Suitable for Hebrew Levels:** Beginners to Intermediate
> **Playing Time:** 5-10 minutes
> **Materials/Resources Needed:** None

Helpful Hints: It is useful to have a vocabulary list to use for this game.

How to play:
The teacher presents a long word in Hebrew, for example: אֶנְצִיקְלוֹפֶּדְיָה (Encyclopedia), or אוּנִיבֶרְסִיטָה (University), etc.

Each student should try to come up with as many words as possible that are "hiding" in this word, using only the Hebrew letters in this long word.

For example, from the long word אֶנְצִיקְלוֹפֶּדְיָה , these words can be formed:

יֶלֶד (boy), יַלְדָה (girl); יָד (hand); קַל (easy); אֵין (there is not); אֳנִיָה (ship); קְלִפָּה (peel); אֵיפֹה (where); אַלוּף (champion); אֲנִי (me); דַף (a page); הוּא (he); הִיא (she); אֵלֶה (these); אִלוּ (if).....

The student who comes up with the most words that "hide" inside the long word wins.

```
אנציקלופדיה
איפה
יוצא
קוף
אני
קל
דף
צל
```

Game No. 27
Can You Unscramble It?

> **Learning Objectives:** Practice Hebrew decoding
> **Suitable for Hebrew Levels:** Beginners
> **Playing Time:** 5-10 minutes
> **Materials/Resources Needed:** None
> **Variations:** The teacher can assign the scrambled word or divide the class into breakout rooms and have the students rotate to solve the riddles.

Helpful Hints: This is a great way to review basic vocabulary.

How to play:

The teacher divides the class into two or three groups. Each group writes one scrambled word for the other group to solve.

Use final letters as hints, for example: ופטלן = טלפון =

First, the teacher should review both original and scrambled words for accuracy.

Switch riddles.

Now, each group gets only two minutes to find the right unscrambled word or phrase.

Start with three-letter words and keep on playing the game, gradually building up to sentences (depending on the Hebrew level of the class).

Game No. 28
From Random Letters to Real Words

> **Learning Objectives:** Practice vocabulary skills in Hebrew
> **Suitable for Hebrew Levels:** Beginners to Intermediate
> **Playing Time:** 5 minutes
> **Materials/Resources Needed:** None

Helpful Hints: A fun game to practice vocabulary Hebrew. Students should have enough Hebrew vocabulary to play this game; hence, it is recommended to play this during the mid-year.

How to play:
The teacher randomly selects eight letters from the Aleph-Bet, e.g., א,י,ש,ת,ח,ס,ר, ע
The students have two minutes to form as many vocabulary words as can be created from those eight letters.

The teacher may share the whiteboard with the annotation option or ask students to write their words on white paper and share it in the video.

Students must have sufficient Hebrew vocabulary to play this game.

From the letters above the following words can be written:

אִישׁ, חָסֵר, יֵשׁ, שַׁי, רַע, רָשָׁע, שַׂר, רַעַשׁ, רֵיחַ, אֵת

Game No. 29
I Spy

> **Learning Objectives:** Practice basic Hebrew vocabulary and conversational skills
> **Suitable for Hebrew Levels:** Beginners to Intermediate
> **Playing Time:** 5-10 minutes
> **Materials/Resources Needed:** None
> **Variations:** Students may describe items visible in their own backgrounds or in the backgrounds of other students.

Helpful Hints: This is a good game to play at the beginning of the lesson as a refresher or a review of vocabulary, including shapes, colors, and items that can be found in the house.

How to play:

There are three ways to play this game:
1) The teacher selects one student to be the "presenter."
The selected student shares his screen. The item needs to be something visible in the video, that is in the background behind the student.
The other students ask the "presenter" questions in Hebrew until they determine the chosen item.
2) The teacher selects one student to be the "presenter."
   The "presenter" chooses one item (visible through the camera) and describes it in Hebrew until the rest of the students figure out the item.
3) The teacher describes an item that is visible through the camera to all, in one of the student's house backgrounds. The students try to figure out the item.

Game No. 30
"Go Fetch!"

Learning Objectives: Practice Hebrew vocabulary
Suitable for Hebrew Levels: Beginners
Playing Time: 5-10 minutes
Materials/Resources Needed: None

Helpful Hints: This game works well as a review of Hebrew vocabulary.

How to play:
The teacher selects one student to be the "Speaker." The "Speaker" calls out a name of a category, for example: יָרֹק (Green), or עָגוּל (Circle).
All students have one minute to go around the house and bring something back related to the category that the speaker called out.
The teacher may want to rotate the "Speaker" role, so everyone gets a turn.

Game No. 31
I Like I Hate

Learning Objectives: Practice conversational Hebrew
Suitable for Hebrew Levels: Beginners to Intermediate
Playing Time: 5-10 minutes
Materials/Resources Needed: None

Helpful Hints: This game works well for practicing conversational skills.

How to play:
Each student writes three things they like and three things they hate.
Students must send it privately via the chat box to the teacher.
The teacher then reads aloud a random statement.
All students need to guess who wrote each statement.

Game No. 32
Show and Tell

> **Learning Objectives:** Practice conversational Hebrew
> **Suitable for Hebrew Levels:** Beginners to Intermediate
> **Playing Time:** 10-15 minutes
> **Materials/Resources Needed:** Each student should have a picture or a real object.

Helpful Hints: This game is an easy way to encourage and spark students' conversations. This game can be used daily as a morning starter or on a weekly basis.

How to play:
The teacher instructs students (in advance) to hold a picture or an item that is important to them.
Each student shares and says something about the item they are holding and why is it important to them.
Other students have permission to react, to support, or to share a positive comment about the item shared.

Game No. 33
Pictionary

> **Learning Objectives:** Practice Hebrew vocabulary or phrases
> **Suitable for Hebrew Levels:** Beginners to Intermediate
> **Playing Time:** 10-15 minutes
> **Materials/Resources Needed:** None
> **Variations:** Use basic Hebrew vocabulary for beginners and more advanced phrases for the advanced levels. Students may also be divided into groups.

Helpful Hints: This game is easy to play. Make sure to enable your screen share option before the meeting.

How to play:
There are two ways to play this game:

1) The teacher shares the whiteboard screen. The teacher starts drawing a picture. Students have one minute to guess the object in the picture and its Hebrew name. The first student to guess correctly wins.

2) The teacher divides the class into two groups. Via the private chat box, the teacher sends the name of the "object" to one "representative" of the group. The representative then has one minute to complete the picture and share the screen. The students in the group need to guess the correct Hebrew word that describes the object.

Variation: For more advanced Hebrew level students, the teacher may want to suggest a phrase or a sentence of a complete scenario.

Game No. 34
Dad Went to the Shuk

> **Learning Objectives:** Practice Hebrew vocabulary
> **Suitable for Hebrew Levels:** Beginners
> **Playing Time:** 10-15 minutes
> **Materials/Resources Needed:** Visual images or none
> **Variations:** Teachers may use visual images or just send the name of the items via the chat box privately.

Helpful Hints: This game works well for review of vocabulary.

How to play:
The teacher presents a visual image on the screen.
The first student says: אַבָּא הוֹלֵךְ לַשׁוּק וְקוֹנֶה (Dad goes to the market and buys). Then, the student adds the name of the item in the picture. For example: אַבָּא הוֹלֵךְ לַשׁוּק וְקוֹנֶה עַגְבָנִיָּה
The next student needs to repeat what the first student said and add another item. For example:
אַבָּא הוֹלֵךְ לַשׁוּק וְקוֹנֶה עַגְבָנִיָּה וּמְלָפְפוֹן (Dad goes to the market and buys a tomato and a cucumber).
The third student repeats what both students said before and adds another item.
The teacher may present the items on the screen so it's easier for everyone to follow, or text the name of the item privately to the students via the chat box. Students should monitor the chat box.
By the time the game gets to the last student, the sentence becomes very long! Items can be fruits, vegetables, meat, fish, soap, etc.

Game No. 35
What's in the Box?

> **Learning Objectives:** Practice Hebrew vocabulary
> **Suitable for Hebrew Levels:** Beginners to Intermediate
> **Playing Time:** 10 minutes
> **Materials/Resources Needed:** Different objects small enough to fit in a box
> **Variations:** Ask a student to describe this object for their friends, all in Hebrew.

Helpful Hints: This is a great way to review basic vocabulary.

How to play:

The teacher hides an object in a box. The teacher then shows the closed box to the students via the video and slightly shakes the box to make noise.

The teacher gives hints in Hebrew to help students figure out the item. Hints may be things like shape, color, what we use it for, what sound it makes, etc.

The students need to guess what's in the box.

Once the item is guessed correctly, the teacher opens the box and presents the item to the class.

The teacher can alternate the items and hide another item in the box.

מה בקופסא?

Game No. 36
Who am I?

Learning Objectives: Practice conversational Hebrew
Suitable for Hebrew Levels: Beginners to Intermediate
Playing Time: 5-10 minutes
Materials/Resources Needed: None

Helpful Hints: This game is fun and easy to play.

How to play:
The teacher instructs all students to turn off their videos but to keep the microphone on.
Each student, in their turn, describe themselves in one or two sentences.
The rest of the students need to guess who was the "hidden speaker."

מי אני ומה שמי?

Game No. 37
Just Act It Out

> **Learning Objectives:** Practice Hebrew vocabulary, words and phrases
> **Suitable for Hebrew Levels:** Beginners to Intermediate
> **Playing Time:** 5-10 minutes
> **Materials/Resources Needed:** None
> **Variations:** Advanced students may act out phrases with multiple words.

Helpful Hints: This game is great for reviewing new vocabulary and phrases.

How to play:
The teacher presents a list of new vocabulary words. Between 10 and 20 words work best for this game. The teacher chooses a volunteer and sends that student a word via the chat box.

The "volunteer" acts out the word in pantomime-like charades. The other students need to guess the word.
Advanced Hebrew level students should act out phrases with three to four words or more.

Game No. 38
Fruit Salad

> **Learning Objectives:** Practice the names of fruit in Hebrew
> **Suitable for Hebrew Levels:** Beginners to Intermediate
> **Playing Time:** 5-10 minutes
> **Materials/Resources Needed:** Visual images of fruits / Students should have a white piece of paper and a pen.
> **Variations:** The game can be played with any vocabulary list category.

Helpful Hints: Keep the visual images of fruits on the screen for everyone to see. Under each image, you should write the name of the fruit so that it's clear.

How to play:
The teacher presents the vocabulary list that includes the names of the fruits next to their matching visual images.

Each student should pick one fruit from the list and write its name on the white piece of paper.

Students should hold the signs in front of the camera.

With eyes closed, the teacher calls out randomly a name of a fruit from the list.

Students who hold the name of the fruit called out by the teacher leave the game/mute themselves.

The teacher keeps reading names of fruits, until the student who picked the last fruit wins.

Variations:
This game can be applied with any vocabulary list category, including transportation, food, symbols, etc.

סלט פירות!

Game No. 39
I'm Sending You a Red Ball. What Can You Send?

Learning Objectives: Practice conversational skills in Hebrew
Suitable for Hebrew Levels: Beginners to Intermediate
Playing Time: 5 minutes
Materials/Resources Needed: None

Helpful Hints: A fun game to practice conversational Hebrew.

How to play:
Students pass a virtual gift to one another and name the virtual gifts.
Each student starts the sentence with: אֲנִי מוֹסֵר לָךְ..., or, אֲנִי מוֹסֶרֶת לָךְ
For example: אֲנִי מוֹסֵר לָךְ כַּדּוּר אָדֹם. מָה אַתְּ מוֹסֶרֶת?
The next student comes up with a different object to pass to a third student and says,
אֲנִי מוֹסֶרֶת לָךְ מִבְרֶשֶׁת שִׁנַּיִם. מָה אַתָּה מוֹסֵר?

Game No. 40
Pet Parade

> **Learning Objectives:** Practice conversational Hebrew
> **Suitable for Hebrew Levels:** Beginners to Intermediate
> **Playing Time:** 10 minutes
> **Materials/Resources Needed:** Each student should bring a real animal, a picture of an animal, or a stuffed animal.
> **Variations:** The teacher may decide to break the session into small discussion rooms. Each room can be divided by the same type of pets, and the discussion leader should have some guiding questions.

Helpful Hints: This game is a great opportunity for students to present their pets via videos while given a chance to talk about their pets. Virtual images or stuffed animals can be presented in a classroom.

How to play:
This game is based on the principles of show and tell.
Students gets a chance to present their pets to the class and to tell their classmates something about their pets. Students may choose to present their real pets or a virtual image of their pets. Younger students may present a stuffed animal. If the teacher chooses to divide the class into small discussion breakout rooms, make sure to assign a "leader" for each room and have some guiding questions.

Game No. 41
5-Second Rule

> **Learning Objectives:** Practice conversational Hebrew and vocabulary
> **Suitable for Hebrew Levels:** Beginners to Intermediate
> **Playing Time:** 5-10 minutes
> **Materials/Resources Needed:** None or visual images
> **Variations:** The teacher may decide to give each student a turn or present an image, and the first student to use the "raise your hand" option wins.

Helpful Hints: This game works well once students gain enough vocabulary to use.

How to play:

The teacher presents a virtual image or calls out a word.

The first student to click the "Raise your hand" button has 20 seconds to say as many words in Hebrew associated with the image presented.

If no student volunteers, the teacher has five seconds to randomly select a student or move on to the next image.

?...מה קשור ל

Game No. 42
No Smiling Now

Learning Objectives: Practice basic vocabulary
Suitable for Hebrew Levels: Beginners
Playing Time: 5-10 minutes
Materials/Resources Needed: Funny virtual images

Helpful Hints: This is a fun and easy game to play at the beginning or end of the lesson.

How to play:
The teacher instructs the students that there is only one rule to this game: No matter what they see on screen: לֹא לִצְחֹק וְלֹא לְחַיֵּךְ (neither laugh nor smile).
The students first repeat the rule after the teacher three or four times.
Then, the teacher shares the screen with some funny pictures or scenarios.
Students who laugh or smile need to mute themselves or leave the game.

Game No. 43
Blind Bingo

> **Learning Objectives:** Practice Hebrew vocabulary
> **Suitable for Hebrew Levels:** Beginners to Intermediate
> **Playing Time:** 15 minutes
> **Materials/Resources Needed:** List of vocabulary words, bingo chart / Teachers should prepare a bingo chart and vocabulary words in advance and send them prior to the lesson.
> **Variations:** During the game, the teacher may call out the vocabulary words or ask questions whereby their answers are one of the vocabulary words.

Helpful Hints: This game is a good review of vocabulary words in writing and understanding the word's meaning.

How to play:

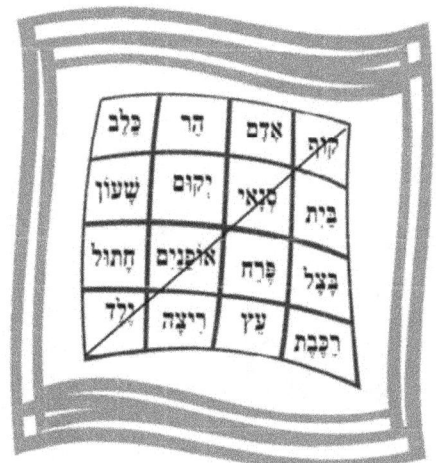

In advance, the teacher sends out a list of vocabulary words and a bingo chart. The list can be sent via email or shared through Google Docs.

If the bingo chart aims for 16 words, then the list of vocabulary should include a total of 25 words.

If the bingo chart aims for 25 words, then the vocabulary list should include 35 total words.

Each student selects 16 (or 25) words to copy into a bingo chart. The students decide the order in which their words will be organized on their chart.

There are two ways to play: The teacher randomly calls out words from the vocabulary list, and students need to fill out a row or a column to call out "Bingo."

The second and more challenging way is when the teacher calls out questions and one of the words on the vocabulary list is the answer. For example: "How do you say a flag in Hebrew?"

Teachers may decide to call out all the words until all students win bingo, or until the first (or the first five students) call out bingo.

Game No. 44
Musical Chairs

Learning Objectives: Practice listening comprehension in Hebrew
Suitable for Hebrew Levels: Beginners
Playing Time: 5-10 minutes
Materials/Resources Needed: YouTube clips in Hebrew
Variations: Multiple instructions may be given to students.

Helpful Hints: This game works well when students need to move around.

How to play:
The teacher instructs the students to circle around their chairs or to walk in place, in front of the camera.
When they hear a specific word pronounced in the song, they need to quickly sit down for a second and then stand up again and keep marching in place.
The teacher then picks a song on YouTube and plays it.
Students must listen carefully to the lyrics of the song and follow the instructions.

כיסאות מוזיקליים

Variations: The teacher may give more than one instruction (e.g., when you hear the word: הַיּוֹם you must sit down, but when you hear the word מָחָר you must raise your hands up).

Game No. 45
Repeat After Me

> **Learning Objectives:** To practice conversational skills in Hebrew
> **Suitable for Hebrew Levels:** Beginners to Intermediate
> **Playing Time:** 5 minutes
> **Materials/Resources Needed:** None

Helpful Hints: This fun game practices conversational Hebrew.

How to play:
The teacher selects one student to be the "Speaker."
The speaker reads a short text that the teacher has sent privately, via the chat box.
The other students repeat exactly what the speaker says without seeing the written text.
The winner is the student who repeats exactly the same words as the speaker does without getting confused.

Game No. 46
Anyone for Spelling?

> **Learning Objectives:** Practice spelling and decoding words in Hebrew
> **Suitable for Hebrew Levels:** Beginners to Intermediate
> **Playing Time:** 10 minutes
> **Materials/Resources Needed:** Students should have paper and pen, or small whiteboards.
> **Variations:** Teachers may call out full sentences and ask for translations.

Helpful Hints: This great game practices and reviews vocabulary words.

How to play:
Students have white paper and pens or small whiteboards with dry erase markers.
The teacher calls out a word and asks students to spell the word correctly.

On the count of three, all students show their papers in the videos.
Students who have the correct spelling get one point.

Students who collect 10 points win the game.
For advanced level, teachers may call out a full sentence or say a sentence in English and ask the students to write the translation in Hebrew, or vice versa.

Games for Intermediate to Advanced Hebrew Levels

Game No. 47
Taboo Words

> **Learning Objectives:** Practice basic conversation and vocabulary words in Hebrew
> **Suitable for Hebrew Levels:** Intermediate to Advanced
> **Playing Time:** 10-15 minutes
> **Materials/Resources Needed:** None / You could use flashcards or write the words on a whiteboard/paper.
> **Variations:** Students may also be asked to answer questions.

Helpful Tips: Make sure the students have enough vocabulary to use instead of the "Taboo" words.

If you are using flashcards or visual images, make sure to put down in writing both the name of the object that needs to be described and the "Taboo" words. It's easier for students to see the object, along with "Taboo" words, without the need to remember. For example, a banana may include the words "yellow" and "fruit" as taboo words. Every object will have its own list of taboo words. Students will remember these "Taboo" words forever.

How to play:
There are two options for playing this game:

Option 1: The teacher presents a visual image (or a flashcard) of an object.
A student volunteers to describe this object to the class without using the "Taboo" words.

For example: Describe תַּפּוּחִים (an apple) without using the words: טוֹב (good) and אֲנִי (I am).

Option 2: The teacher or a "volunteer" asks each student a question in turn. Each student answers the question without using the agreed upon "Taboo" words.
If you are not using flashcards, you should simply write the taboo words on the board. Taboo words for this option could be, for example: "And," Color", "It's", or other words of your choosing.

Game No. 48
It's Trivia Time

> **Learning Objectives:** Practice Hebrew vocabulary
> **Suitable for Hebrew Levels:** Intermediate to Advanced
> **Playing Time:** 15 minutes
> **Materials/Resources Needed:** Use PowerPoint slides or write the questions on a whiteboard/paper.
> **Variations:** There are two ways to play this game: The teacher can ask a question and students answer, or the teacher can give the answers and students ask the questions (like in "Jeopardy").

Helpful Tips: Make sure you have enough questions for every student in the class. Group representatives cannot be used more than once; therefore, all students get a turn to answer a question.

How to play:

The teacher divides the class into two groups. Choose boys vs. girls, groups divided by last names, birthdays or divide the class in the way you prefer.

Each group selects a representative to answer one question. Each question has a different sum of points depending on how difficult the question is. If the answer is correct, the group gets the points; otherwise the other group gets a chance to "steal" the question.

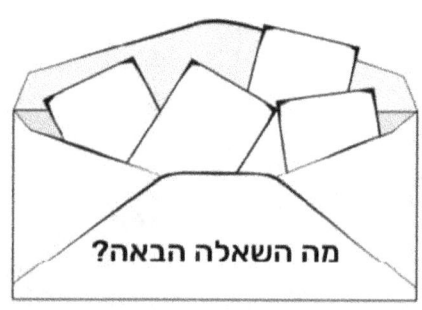

Questions can be, for example: "How do you say … in Hebrew," "What's the plural of …," "Translate the following sentence from English to Hebrew," etc.

Alternatively, if the teacher decides to play the game as "Jeopardy," make sure to use statements like: "He was the visionary of the revival of the modern Hebrew language." Questions may be in any subject area.

The "representatives" should be rotated and allowed to consult with their groups for the correct answers.

Game No. 49
The Rush for Wiki

> **Learning Objectives:** Practice reading/writing skills in Hebrew
> **Levels:** Intermediate to Advanced
> **Playing Time:** 5-10 minutes
> **Materials/Resources Needed:** None. Teacher may want to prepare questions in advance.
> **Variations:** Teacher may prepare the questions or instruct students to come up with questions in advance.

Helpful Hints: Make sure students have access to Google or any other search engine.

How to play:
The teacher asks a "research question," for example, "Who can tell me, how many types of תפוחים are there?"
Then, the students rush to search Google or Wiki (depending on the question) and the first student to come back with the correct answer in Hebrew wins a point.

Game No. 50
Can Google Translate it?

> **Learning objectives:** Practice reading/writing skills in Hebrew
> **Suitable for Hebrew Levels:** Intermediate to Advanced
> **Playing Time:** 5-10 minutes
> **Materials/Resources Needed:** None
> **Variations:** Teachers may prepare the questions or instruct students to come up with their own questions in advance.

Helpful Hints: Make sure students have access to Google on the Internet.

How to play:
There are a few options to play this game:
1. The teacher calls out a sentence in Hebrew or English, and the first student to type it into Google Translate and reads it back to the teacher, is the winner.

2. The student says a word in Hebrew followed by a sentence. The word should be one that has more than one correct meaning when translated. The students need to know which of the translations suggested by Google will be the right one for this specific sentence.

For Example: The word is: יָמִים (it has two meanings, days or oceans)

The sentence is: "When I look at the map, I see many יָמִים"

Voice option on Google Translate – The teacher types a sentence and shares the screen with the students. Then, the students use the voice input on Google Translate and read the sentence aloud asking for Google to translate it either from Hebrew to English or English to Hebrew. The first student to get the translated sentence has to read it back to the teacher.

Game No. 51
The Last Word

Learning Objectives: To practice conversational Hebrew
Suitable for Hebrew Levels: Intermediate to Advanced
Playing Time: 5-10 minutes
Materials/Resources Needed: None

Helpful Hints: This game works well in keeping students' attention.

How to play:
The teacher asks one student to say any sentence in Hebrew. The other students must listen very carefully. Once the first student completes the first sentence, the next student must start a new sentence using the last word that the first student used.
To make this game easier to follow, the teacher may want to write each sentence said on the whiteboard and underline the last word.
For example:

בְּכָל יוֹם שְׁלִישִׁי אֲנִי הוֹלֶכֶת לַיָם.
בַּיָם אֲנִי שׂוֹחָה בְּמַיִם וְאוֹכֶלֶת גְלִידָה.
גְלִידָה הִיא כָּל כָּךְ טְעִימָה.

Game No. 52
Would you rather ... ?

> **Learning Objectives:** Practice conversational Hebrew
> **Suitable for Hebrew Levels:** Intermediate
> **Playing Time:** 5-10 minutes
> **Materials/Resources Needed:** None/ Teacher may want to prepare questions in advance
> **Variations:** May be played as poll or ice breaker

Helpful Hints: This game is fun to play and is great for listening comprehension and sparking conversations.

האם אתה מעדיף לשחות בבריכה או בים?

How to play:
The teacher starts by asking each student a question:
Would you rather do that or that?   **הַאִם אַתָּה מַעֲדִיף?**
The teacher then offers two scenarios that can be funny, offbeat, or thought-provoking.
For example: Would you rather be bald or be too hairy?
Each student has a chance to select one of two possible scenarios. Teachers may ask students to explain why they chose this scenario.
Variations: This game may also be played as a poll or ice breaker.

Game No. 53
Never Have I Ever ...

> **Learning Objectives:** Practice conversational Hebrew
> **Suitable for Hebrew Levels:** Intermediate
> **Playing Time:** 5-10 minutes
> **Materials/Resources Needed:** None or white paper with Yes or No printed on either side
> **Variations:** Use flags instead of fingers

Helpful Hints: Instruct students to be honest while playing this game. Keep the statements simple and try to make your statements funny.

How to play:
Students should hold up 10 fingers.

The teacher starts reading or calling out statements. Students who have done the activity mentioned should put one finger down.

Students who put down all their fingers are eliminated from the game.

The winner of the game is the last remaining student with a finger raised.

Variations:
Instead of using fingers, students may use flags with the words כן on one side and לא on the other side and present the flags in the video when the statement is read out loud.

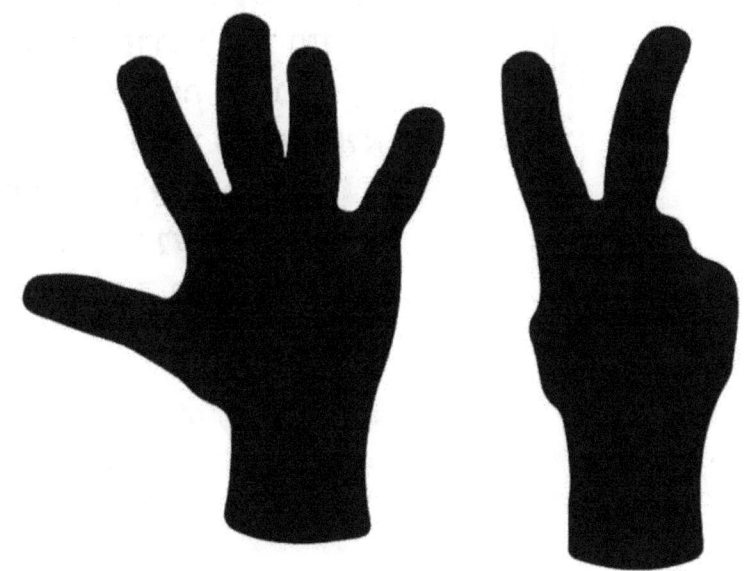

NEVER HAVE I EVER .... EXAMPLES

מֵעוֹלָם לֹא... דוּגְמָאוֹת

1. הָיִיתִי מְאֹהָב
2. צָבַעְתִּי אֶת הַשֵּׂעָר
3. שָׁבַרְתִּי עֶצֶם בַּגּוּף
4. בָּנִיתִי מַשֶּׁהוּ מֵעֵץ
5. צָרַחְתִּי בְּמַהֲלָךְ סֶרֶט מַפְחִיד
6. בִּקַּרְתִּי בְּאֵרוּעַ סְפּוֹרְט מִקְצוֹעִי
7. יָשַׁנְתִּי עַד הַצָּהֳרַיִם
8. פָּתַחְתִּי מִכְתָּב אוֹ מַתָּנָה לַמְרוֹת שֶׁאָמְרוּ לִי לֹא לִפְתֹּחַ
9. צָחַקְתִּי כָּל כָּךְ עַד שֶׁבָּרַח לִי פִּיפִי
10. שָׂרַפְתִּי אֶת עַצְמִי בְּמַגְהֵץ אוֹ עִם גַּפְרוּר
11. אָכַלְתִּי אֹכֶל שֶׁנָּפַל עַל הָרִצְפָּה
12. חָלַקְתִּי סֶנְדְּוִיץ' עִם הַכֶּלֶב שֶׁלִּי
13. הָיִיתִי חוֹלָה בְּיוֹם הַהֻלֶּדֶת שֶׁלִּי
14. נָעַלְתִּי אֶת הַמַּפְתְּחוֹת שֶׁלִּי בָּרֶכֶב
15. נִכְנַס לִי זְבוּב קָטָן לַפֶּה, לָאַף אוֹ לָעַיִן
16. הֵעִירוּ לִי בַּסִּפְרִיָּה כִּי עָשִׂיתִי רַעַשׁ
17. טִפַּסְתִּי עַל עֵץ אֲבָל פָּחַדְתִּי לָרֶדֶת חֲזָרָה
18. נִשְׁפַּךְ עָלַי קָפֶה לִפְנֵי פְּגִישָׁה חֲשׁוּבָה
19. שָׁבַרְתִּי בְּטָעוּת מַשֶּׁהוּ בַּבַּיִת שֶׁל חָבֵר וְלֹא סִפַּרְתִּי לוֹ
20. שָׁלַחְתִּי הוֹדָעַת טֶקְסְט לְאָדָם הַלֹּא נָכוֹן
21. הִדְבַּקְתִּי מַסְטִיק מִתַּחַת לַשֻּׁלְחָן
22. הִפַּלְתִּי אֶת הַטֶּלֶפוֹן הַנַּיָּד בְּטָעוּת לַשֵּׁרוּתִים

Game No. 54
A Surprise Riddle

> **Learning Objectives:** Review Hebrew vocabulary or spelling skills
> **Suitable for Hebrew Levels:** Intermediate to Advanced
> **Playing Time:** 5-10 minutes
> **Materials/Resources Needed:** Teachers should prepare in advance small flashcards or PowerPoint slides with riddles

Helpful Hints: A great game to practice and review vocabulary words or grammar.

How to play:
The teacher prepares in advance question cards with riddles in Hebrew or separate slides in Hebrew.

Question cards may be on a variety of subjects that students have already learned. The riddles can be easy as refreshers or more advanced.

In the middle of the lesson, at an appropriate moment to do so, the teacher pulls out a random question card and shares the screen.

Question cards can be, for example, "What is the singular of נָשִׁים?" or "How do you say in Hebrew 10 tables?", etc.

SURPRISE RIDDLES   חִידוֹת בְּהַפְתָּעָה

A Surprise Riddle 1

Complete the following sentence:

יַלְדָּה יָפָה
יְלָדוֹת יָפוֹת
עִיר גְּדוֹלָה
_____ גְּדוֹלוֹת

A Surprise Riddle 2

Solve the riddle:

צָרִיךְ פֶּה כְּדֵי לְדַבֵּר
וְאַף כְּדֵי לְהָרִיחַ
אָזְנַיִם בִּשְׁבִיל לִשְׁמֹעַ
וּמָה כְּדֵי לִרְאוֹת ?

A Surprise Riddle 3

Solve the riddle:

מָה אֶפְשָׁר לִשְׁמֹעַ אַךְ לֹא לִרְאוֹת?

(תְּשׁוּבָה: קוֹל)

A Surprise Riddle 4

Solve the riddle:

אֲנִי מַחְזִיק הַרְבֵּה מַיִם, לַמְרוֹת שֶׁיֵּשׁ בִּי הַרְבֵּה חוֹרִים.
מִי אֲנִי?

(תְּשׁוּבָה: סְפוֹג)

A Surprise Riddle 5

Solve the riddle:

אֲנִי גָּר בַּבַּיִת לְבַדִּי
וּכְשֶׁאֲנִי רוֹצֶה לָצֵאת הַחוּצָה
אֲנִי שׁוֹבֵר אֶת כָּל הַקִּירוֹת....
מִי אֲנִי?

(תְּשׁוּבָה: אֶפְרוֹחַ בְּתוֹךְ בֵּיצָה)

A Surprise Riddle 6

Answer the question:

מָה הַשָּׁעָה עַכְשָׁיו?

Game No. 55
Take a Poll

> **Learning Objectives:** Practice reading comprehension
> **Suitable for Hebrew Levels:** Intermediate to Advanced
> **Playing Time:** 5 minutes
> **Materials/Resources Needed:** None / Teachers may want to prepare poll questions in advance
> **Variations:** This game can be used for reading comprehension of short sentences or to get input on the lesson

Helpful Hints: This game is great for practicing reading comprehension with short sentences or as an ice breaker.

How to play:

In advance of the lesson, the teacher sets up poll questions for the students to take during class. Poll questions may include short refresher questions, like "How do you say in Hebrew…?" or a short text in Hebrew that students need to read and select the correct answer from the multiple-choice options.

Teachers could use more than one poll during the lesson.

In many platforms like Zoom, the poll option is already built in, or you could use other platforms like polleverywhere.com.

Game No. 56
Annotation for All

> **Learning Objectives:** Practice writing in Hebrew
> **Suitable for Hebrew Levels:** Intermediate
> **Playing Time:** 10 minutes
> **Materials/Resources Needed:** None/A virtual image

Helpful Hints: This fun game practices collaboration and Hebrew writing

How to play:
The teacher selects an image with many details, like a farm, a market, a busy bus stop, a train station, etc.
The teacher shares the screen with the students.
The annotation option should be enabled for all students to use.
Ask students to use the annotation pen and to write each item's name next to it in Hebrew.

The teacher has control of all writing and can correct any spelling mistakes.
Students may use print or script letters.

Game No. 57
Say It in Words

> **Learning Objectives:** Practice conversational Hebrew
> **Suitable for Hebrew Levels:** Intermediate to Advanced
> **Playing Time:** 5-10 minutes
> **Materials/Resources Needed:** Visual images of emojis
> **Variations:** For beginners, use simple and basic emojis; for advanced levels, use more complex emojis that express feelings, abstracts, or actions.
> You may also create complete phrases or sentences expressed by emojis only and ask students to guess the phrase hidden behind those symbols.

Helpful Hints: This game works well after teaching the Hebrew vocabulary words to express emotions or as a refresher of a variety of topics.

How to play:
The teacher sends a phrase to one of the students via the chat box.
By using the annotation and sharing their screens, the students use emojis only to express the phrase.
The rest of the students should guess the phrase from the expression.

Variations: For beginners, the teacher may present an emoji on the screen and ask students to say or write the first word in Hebrew that comes to mind describing this emoji.

Advanced Hebrew students may write a sentence or come up with a whole imaginative story based on one emoji or more.

FROM PHRASES TO EMOJIS — מִפְתָגָמִים לְאִימוֹגִ'ים

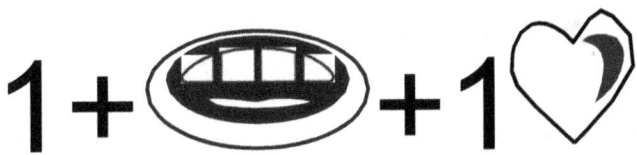 אֶחָד בַּפֶּה וְאֶחָד בַּלֵּב

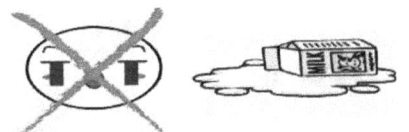 לֹא בּוֹכִים עַל חָלָב שֶׁנִּשְׁפַּךְ

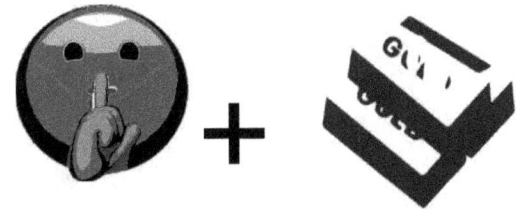 שְׁתִיקָה שָׁוָה זָהָב

 לֹא דֻּבִּים וְלֹא יַעַר

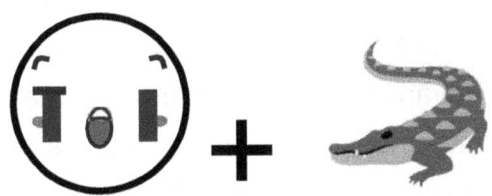 דִּמְעוֹת תַּנִּין

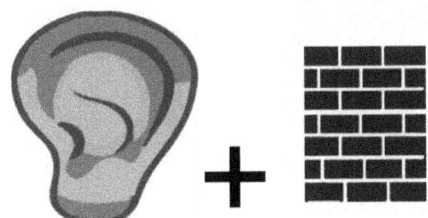 אָזְנַיִם לַכֹּתֶל

 הַקַּשׁ שֶׁשָּׁבַר אֶת גַּב הַגָּמָל

Game No. 58
The Five Senses

> **Learning Objectives:** Practice Hebrew vocabulary
> **Suitable for Hebrew Levels:** Intermediate to Advanced
> **Playing Time:** 5-10 minutes
> **Materials/Resources Needed:** White paper and pens
> **Variations:** Use the annotation option on the whiteboard

How to play:

Each student should have a piece of paper and a pencil.

Alternatively, use the annotation option and write the categories on the whiteboard.

The teacher asks the students to write down (without talking or sharing ideas) everything they can hear, see, smell, taste, or touch around them in the house.

When done, have the students share their ideas.

Beginner students may use basic Hebrew vocabulary, while more advanced Hebrew students may use full sentences, abstracts terms, paragraphs, etc.

Game No. 59
Fortunately, or Unfortunately

> **Learning Objectives:** Practice conversational Hebrew
> **Suitable for Hebrew Levels:** Intermediate
> **Playing Time:** 5-10 minutes
> **Materials/Resources Needed:** None
> **Variations:** This game can be played through writing

Helpful Hints: This game works well for practicing conversational skills.

למזלי לצערי   לשמחתי

How to play:

The teacher "browses" the videos and selects one student to be in the "spotlight."

The chosen student provides an opening sentence in Hebrew. Then, the teacher "browses" again and picks another student to be in the "spotlight" who completes the sentence, using either "Fortunately" (luckily) **לְמַזְלִי** or "Unfortunately" **לְצַעֲרִי**.

For example, one student might say:

"אֶתְמוֹל הָלַכְתִּי לַחֲנוּת כְּדֵי לִקְנוֹת חוּלְצָה חֲדָשָׁה"

(Yesterday, I went to the store in order to buy a new shirt).

The other student could then add:

"לְמַזְלִי, הַחֲנוּת הָיְתָה סְגוּרָה, כִּי אֲנִי שׂוֹנֵא לִקְנוֹת בְּגָדִים"

(Luckily, the store was closed, because I hate buying clothes).

Advanced Hebrew level students can keep on taking turns and make it into a story.

Variations: You can play this game in writing via the chat box, where the first student writes down the opening sentence and their friends continue the story.

Game No. 60
This is the Voice ...

Learning Objectives: Practice conversational Hebrew
Suitable for Hebrew Levels: Intermediate to Advanced
Playing Time: 10 minutes
Materials/Resources Needed: None

Helpful Hints: This great game sparks conversations.

How to play:

All students mute themselves and turn off their videos.

Three students are chosen to sing or read a short text in Hebrew.

All students act as judges. If they like the reading fluency of the student, they turn on their camera. If they don't like it, they stay muted.

At the end of each round, all judges (even those who did not turn on their cameras) must provide positive feedback to the performer.

All this conversation should be conducted in Hebrew.

Game No. 61
Are you smarter than ...?

Learning Objectives: To practice Hebrew skills
Suitable for Hebrew Levels: Intermediate to Advanced
Playing Time: 10 minutes
Materials/Resources Needed: Students should have a parent with them/ Questions should be prepared in advance

Helpful Hints: Have a few adults represent the parents' group and the same number of students to represent the students' group. You can rotate between adults and students, so everyone has a chance to participate.

How to play:

The teacher selects three or four students and three or four parents to compete. Everyone else is quiet.

The teacher asks the first question aimed at the parents' group. The parents have 60 seconds to answer. If they know the correct answer, they win one point. If they don't know the answer, the question goes to the students' group. If the students know the answer, they win one point.

The teacher then keeps asking questions until the first group of parents or students wins all 10 points.

Questions may be related to anything that students have already learned in Hebrew, including vocabulary, translation, grammar, etc.

Game No. 62
There are 50 ways to ... Part 1

Learning Objectives: Practice writing in Hebrew skills
Suitable for Hebrew Levels: Intermediate to Advanced
Playing Time: 10 minutes
Materials/Resources Needed: None
Variations: To make it more challenging, time it

Helpful Hints: For this fun collaborative online game, enable students with the option to use the annotation markers prior to the start of the session.

How to play:
The teacher writes a question and shares the whiteboard screen with the students.

The question should start with: "There are 50 ways to …"
The teacher then adds a topic, like: "There are 50 ways to welcome a new student," or "There are 50 ways to say תּוֹדָה וּלְהִתְרָאוֹת."
Upon an agreed signal, the students, using the annotation option, write their input on the board to answer the question.
To make it more fun and challenging, this game can be timed. Students have two minutes to come up with their own creative ideas to answer the question; however, students may not repeat something that someone already wrote.

Game No. 63
There are 50 ways to ... Part 2

Learning Objectives: Practice Hebrew comprehension skills
Suitable for Hebrew Levels: Intermediate to Advanced
Playing Time: 5 minutes
Materials/Resources Needed: None

Helpful Hints: This is a fun game to combine creative thinking while checking Hebrew comprehension skills.

How to play:

The teacher calls out an instruction. The instruction must begin with the sentence: "There are 50 ways to ..." For example: "There are 50 ways לָשֶׁבֶת עַל כִּיסֵא (to sit on a chair)." Students should follow the instruction given but may not repeat something that someone already did. For example, one student may sit on the chair, back to the camera, while another turns the chair upside down.

Another example: The teacher calls out, "There are 50 ways to לְקַפֵּל אֶת הַדַּף (fold the paper)." Students fold a paper in different ways without repeating another student's way of folding.

רַעֲיוֹנוֹת לְמִשְׂחָק: "יֵשׁ 50 דְּרָכִים"
IDEAS FOR THE GAME: "THERE ARE 50 WAYS TO"

There are 50 ways to fold napkins	יֵשׁ 50 דְּרָכִים לְקַפֵּל מַפִּיּוֹת
There are 50 ways to write a song	יֵשׁ 50 דְּרָכִים לִכְתֹּב שִׁיר
There are 50 ways to say I love you	יֵשׁ 50 דְּרָכִים לוֹמַר שֶׁאֲנִי אוֹהֵב אוֹתָךְ
There are 50 ways to light a candle	יֵשׁ 50 דְּרָכִים לְהַדְלִיק נֵר
There are 50 ways to save money	יֵשׁ 50 דְּרָכִים לַחֲסֹךְ כֶּסֶף
There are 50 ways to step into a pool	יֵשׁ 50 דְּרָכִים לְהִכָּנֵס לַבְּרֵכָה
There are 50 ways to open a letter	יֵשׁ 50 דְּרָכִים לִפְתֹּחַ מִכְתָּב
There are 50 ways to say hello	יֵשׁ 50 דְּרָכִים לוֹמַר שָׁלוֹם
There are 50 ways to wear a hat	יֵשׁ 50 דְּרָכִים לַחֲבֹשׁ כּוֹבַע
There are 50 ways to make pasta	יֵשׁ 50 דְּרָכִים לְהָכִין פַּסְטָה
There are 50 ways to watch a movie	יֵשׁ 50 דְּרָכִים לִצְפּוֹת בַּסֶּרֶט
There are 50 ways to ride a bike	יֵשׁ 50 דְּרָכִים לִרְכֹּב עַל אוֹפַנַּיִם
There are 50 ways to draw a cat	יֵשׁ 50 דְּרָכִים לְצַיֵּר חָתוּל
There are 50 ways to wash your face	יֵשׁ 50 דְּרָכִים לִשְׁטֹף אֶת הַפָּנִים
There are 50 ways to eat cookies	יֵשׁ 50 דְּרָכִים לֶאֱכֹל עוּגִיּוֹת

Game No. 64
Not your typical Mafia man

> **Learning Objectives:** Practice conversational skills in Hebrew
> **Suitable for Hebrew Levels:** Intermediate to Advanced
> **Playing Time:** 5-10 minutes
> **Materials/Resources Needed:** None

Helpful Hints: This fun game practices conversational Hebrew.

How to play:

The teacher selects one student to act as the מְסַפֵּר סִפּוּרִים (storyteller).

The storyteller privately, via the chat box, appoints someone to be the מַאפְיָה (Mafia) and asks that person who will be dead in the story.

The storyteller then appoints two wizards to protect the Mafia man; however, one קוֹסֵם (wizard) is good and one קוֹסֵם (wizard) is bad.

Next, the storyteller privately, via chat box, appoints the בַּלָּשׁ (the detective), who needs to guess the identity of the Mafia man.

The storyteller starts telling a story about a crime that took place.

The detective needs to convince everyone of the identity of the Mafia man.

The good wizard needs to defend the person suspected of being the Mafia man, while the bad wizard tries to incriminate someone else of being the Mafia man.

Who is right? Only the rest of the students can decide.

Game No. 65
Walking on Google Maps

Learning Objectives: Practice vocabulary words in Hebrew
Suitable for Hebrew Levels: Intermediate
Playing Time: 5 minutes
Materials/Resources Needed: None

Helpful Hints: This fun game helps students review directions in Hebrew.

ישר ישר ישר   ישר עד הצומת

How to play:

The teacher instructs students to open Google Maps on their computers and locate their houses.

Using instructions given by the teacher, students start "walking" on the maps.

For example, the teacher may say:

לֵךְ קָדִימָה שְׁלוֹשָׁה רְחוֹבוֹת. פְּנֵה שְׂמֹאלָה וְהַמְשֵׁךְ לָלֶכֶת יָשָׁר עַד שֶׁתַּגִּיעַ לְצֹמֶת רָאשִׁית. בַּצֹּמֶת פְּנֵה יָמִינָה וְלֵךְ יָשָׁר עוֹד חֲמִשָּׁה בָּתִּים. מְצָא אֶת הַמִּסְעָדָה הַקְּרוֹבָה.

When the game is done, students take a screenshot or share their screens to see where they each landed.

Game No. 66
You've Got Mail!

Learning Objectives: Practice conversational Hebrew
Suitable for Hebrew Levels: Intermediate to Advanced
Playing Time: 5-10 minutes
Materials/Resources Needed: None

Helpful Tips: Teacher should instruct the students to keep an eye on their chat box.

How to play:
During the lesson, the teacher randomly sends messages to the students via the chat box.

Students should monitor their chat box and once they received the message, they have two minutes to respond. Teachers may send simple questions like: "Jacob, type in your name in Hebrew" or "Yael — if you see this message, you have two minutes to tell us a joke."

Messages can be in the format of a hidden code. For example: "In Gematria, the letter Aleph is one point and the letter Bet is two points. How many points total for the word: אַבָּא?"

Game No. 67
The Echo

Learning Objectives: Practice conversational skills
Suitable for Hebrew Levels: Intermediate to Advanced
Playing Time: 5-10 minutes
Materials/Resources Needed: None

Helpful Hints: This game is great as an ice breaker.

How to play:
The teacher chooses one student to go first.
The teacher asks the student three questions:

?אֵיפֹה הוּא גָּר

?אֵיךְ קוֹרְאִים לְאָח אוֹ אָחוֹת שֶׁלּוֹ

?מָה הוּא אוֹהֵב לַעֲשׂוֹת בַּזְּמַן הַפָּנוּי

The teacher then randomly points to another student in class.

The first student selected, needs to answer those three questions regarding the second student the teacher pointed at. If any of the answers are not correct, a third student is appointed to assist.

Game No. 68
A Random Word

> **Learning Objectives:** Practice Conversational Hebrew
> **Suitable for Hebrew Levels:** Intermediate
> **Playing Time:** 5-10 minutes
> **Materials/Resources Needed:** None

Helpful Hints: This is a good game for practicing Hebrew speaking skills.

How to play:
The teacher sends a random word privately to one of the students via chat box.

Then, the teacher asks this student a question out loud, which must be answered. The student must insert this word (sent via the chat box) at least three times into the reply.

After the student answers the question, all students must guess what was the "inserted word."

For example: The teacher sends the word "שָׁמַיִם" to a random student via the chat box. Then, the teacher asks: "Ron, can you tell me: מָה מֶזֶג הָאֲוִויר הַיּוֹם ?"

The student may say:

הַיּוֹם יֵשׁ שֶׁמֶשׁ בַּשָּׁמַיִם. הַיּוֹם בַּשָּׁמַיִם אֵין עֲנָנִים. הַשָּׁמַיִם כְּחוּלִים וְיָפִים

Game No. 69
Animal or Object?

> **Learning Objectives:** Practice Hebrew vocabulary
> **Suitable for Hebrew Levels:** Intermediate to Advanced
> **Playing Time:** 15-20 minutes
> **Materials/Resources Needed:** None or white paper

Helpful Hints: This is a challenging game.

How to play:

One student starts by reciting the Aleph-Bet until another student says: עֲצוֹר (Stop). When the student says עֲצוֹר , the letter "landed on" is the chosen letter for this round. The teacher draws a table on the whiteboard and shares the screen with the following categories:

- ❖ Animals
- ❖ Place
- ❖ Objects
- ❖ Name
- ❖ Food ... and so on

By using the annotation tool, or by typing into the chat box, the students fill out the table on the board with words that match a category and begin with the letter selected.

For example: If the letter is Yud:

Place: יִשְׂרָאֵל (Israel)
Animal: יַנְשׁוּף (Owl)
Object: יָרֵחַ (Moon);
Name: יְהוּדָה (Yehuda);
Food: יוֹגוּרט (Yogurt).

Game No. 70
It's One Long Story After All

> **Learning Objectives:** Practice conversational Hebrew
> **Suitable for Hebrew Levels:** Intermediate to Advanced
> **Playing Time:** 5-10 minutes
> **Materials/Resources Needed:** None
> **Variations:** Begin the story at the end.

Helpful Hints: This game is fun to play at the beginning of the class or closer to the end of the lesson to keep students' attention.

How to play:
All students' microphones are muted. The teacher starts telling a story in Hebrew. Then, the teacher "browses" the videos and selects one student to be unmuted. The student who was selected continues the story, until muted and the teacher moves on to the next student to be unmuted.

Variations:
The teacher may choose to begin telling the story from the end of the story, asking the students to tell what happened before.

Game No. 71
What's Your Word?

> **Learning Objectives:** Practice Hebrew vocabulary
> **Suitable for Hebrew Levels:** Intermediate to Advanced
> **Playing Time:** 5-10 minutes
> **Materials/Resources Needed:** White paper
> **Variations:** Limit words to a specific category.

Helpful Hints: This game works well as a refresher or review of vocabulary.

How to play:

Each student should have a white piece of paper and a marker or a pen.

When the teacher calls מָה הַמִּילָה שֶׁלְךָ? "What's your Word?" the students write down on the paper one word of their choosing.

On an agreed signal, the teacher calls מִילִים אֵלַי בְּבַקָשָׁה and all students present their words to the camera. The teacher can see if there are any spelling errors or similar words.

Variations:

The teacher may decide to use only "words" that belong to a specific category. For example, the teacher may say: "Today, we're only going to use words that belong to the category: Things you can find in the kitchen."

Game No. 72
The Funniest Joke

> **Learning Objectives:** Practice conversational Hebrew
> **Suitable for Hebrew Levels:** Intermediate to Advanced
> **Playing Time:** 10 minutes
> **Materials/Resources Needed:** None
> **Variation:** Students may want to prepare jokes in advance.

Helpful Hints: This game is fun and helps students practice their Hebrew conversational skills.

How to play:
Each student has a turn to tell a favorite funniest joke.
Jokes should be limited to under 30 seconds.
The funniest joke, voted by students, wins!

Game No. 73
Advertise it

> **Learning Objectives:** Practice conversational Hebrew
> **Suitable for Hebrew Levels:** Intermediate
> **Playing Time:** 5-10 minutes
> **Materials/Resources Needed:** Small items or visual photos
> **Variations:** Students can work in small groups or individually (via breakout rooms).

Helpful Hints: This game is good to conclude the lesson.

How to play:
The teacher selects a random item, for example a math book.
Students have a couple of minutes to come up with a creative way to advertise this item and convince the audience why they should buy it.
Advertisements may be in the format of slogans, memes, or short poems in rhymes.

ונעבור לפרסומות

Game No. 74
True or Not?

> **Learning Objectives:** Practice conversational Hebrew
> **Suitable for Hebrew Levels:** Intermediate to Advanced
> **Playing Time:** 10-15 minutes
> **Materials/Resources Needed:** None
> **Variations:** The number of sentences may be increased or restricted to a specific category.

Helpful Hints: This game may take longer. I recommend selecting four or five students to play the game and let the other students be the guessers.

How to play:
Ask the students to think of two sentences to describe themselves.
One sentence must be true, but the other sentence must be false. The rest of the students try to guess which one of the sentences is the **true** one.
Of course, all sentences are spoken in Hebrew.

Variations:
The teacher may instruct students to share three sentences, totaling two true sentences and one false or vice versa; be clear about this rule prior to playing this game.
Teachers may instruct students to use all sentences related to a specific category (e.g., all sentences should be related to daily life, your family, etc.).

Game No. 75
What Else Can We Make?

> **Learning Objectives:** Practice conversational Hebrew
> **Suitable for Hebrew Levels:** Intermediate to Advanced
> **Playing Time:** 10 minutes
> **Materials/Resources Needed:** Visual images of places and objects

Helpful Hints: This game inspires creativity, as well as conversation.

How to play:

The teacher presents different objects or visual images of various objects.

The teacher asks: מָה עוֹד אֶפְשָׁר לַעֲשׂוֹת עִם זֶה   What else can you use it for?

For example, items can be:

גּוּמִיָּה (Rubber band)

גַּלְגַּל (Wheel)

זְכוּכִית מַגְדֶּלֶת (Magnifying glass)

חַלּוֹן (Window)

Students who come up with the most creative answers win points.

Game No. 76
What's My Role?

> **Learning Objectives:** Practice conversational Hebrew
> **Suitable for Hebrew Levels:** Intermediate to Advanced
> **Playing Time:** 5-10 minutes
> **Materials/Resources Needed:** None
> **Variations:** This game can be played as one group or in small groups. For each group, assign a leader. Roles may also be limited to focused categories.

Helpful Hints: The teacher's role is more active in this game. Teachers may want to choose different assigned leaders to give students a chance to be more active.

How to play:
Via the chat box, students must decide on one "role" to be assigned to the teacher or leader. For example, the teacher's role is a "Milkman."
The teacher should not look at the chat box at this time.
Then, the teacher asks various questions in order to guess the assigned "role."
If the class is divided into small discussion groups, each group selects a "Leader" and assigns that person a "role." The "Leader" then needs to guess the "role" by asking the other students questions.
The class teacher can be a supervisor and visit each discussion room to monitor.

Variations:
The teacher may instruct the group to select a role related to a specific category, for example: "Roles you can only find in Israel."

ובתפקיד החלבן קבלו את...

Game No. 77
A Quick Draw

> **Learning Objectives:** Practice Hebrew phrases
> **Suitable for Hebrew Levels:** Intermediate
> **Playing Time:** 5-10 minutes
> **Materials/Resources Needed:** Students should have white paper and a pen

Helpful Hints: This game provides a quick review of Hebrew vocabulary.

How to play:
The teacher picks a sentence or a phrase and says it out loud.
Each student has one minute to express this sentence or phrase by drawing it on the paper.

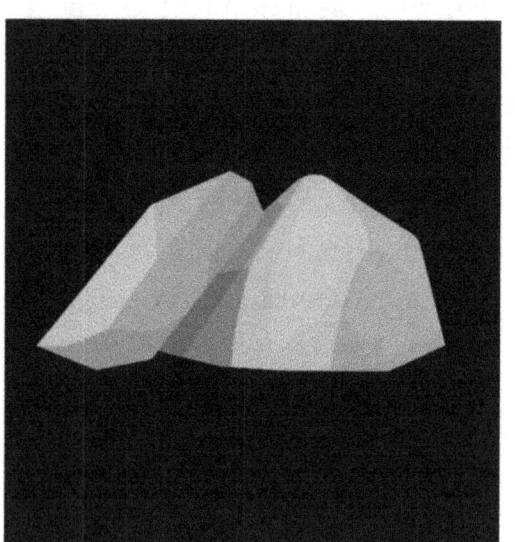

The teacher asks the students to share their artwork or screen and explain why they chose to express the phrase in that way.
For example: Ask students to draw their meaning to the phrase: " וְאָהַבְתָּ לְרֵעֲךָ כָּמוֹךָ".

חזק כמו סלע

Game No. 78
What's Wrong?

> **Learning Objectives:** Practice Hebrew spelling or grammar
> **Suitable for Hebrew Levels:** Intermediate
> **Playing Time:** 5-10 minutes
> **Materials/Resources Needed:** None
> **Variations:** Use simple sentences or basic words for beginners and more complex ones for advanced students.

Helpful Hints: The inserted "Errors" can be basic, hidden or obvious, depending on the class level.

How to play:
The teacher writes a few sentences in Hebrew on the screen and shares the screen with the class.
However, the teacher **deliberately** inserts some "Errors" into the sentences shared with the students.
Errors can be in spelling, in grammar, in tenses, etc.
By using the annotation option, students have 30 seconds to circle the errors and suggest the right way to correct them.

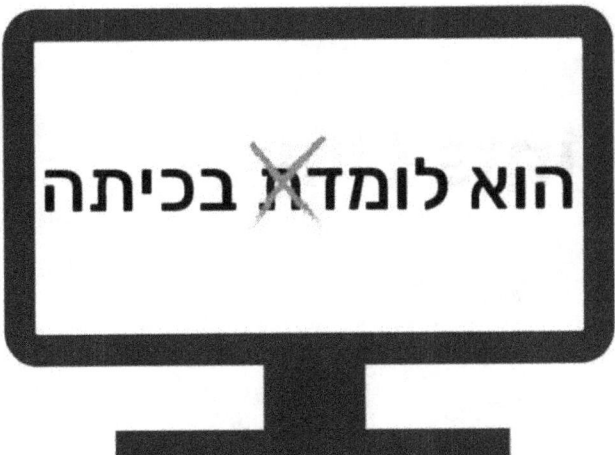

Game No. 79
Describe it for me, please

> **Learning Objectives:** Practice conversational Hebrew
> **Suitable for Hebrew Levels:** Intermediate
> **Playing Time:** 5-10 minutes
> **Materials/Resources Needed:** None

Helpful Hints: This is a fun and energizing game.

How to play:

The teacher appoints a student to be in charge and leaves the session for two minutes. In the meantime, the group decides on a rarely used object, for example: Whistling kettle קוּמְקוּם שׁוֹרֵק

When returning to the session, the teacher needs to guess the object.

The students provide 15 hints to describe the object without saying the name of the object itself, or any words that may be included in the phrase.

The teacher only has five guesses to try to come up with the right answer.

15 Hints Only

מה זה?

Game No. 80
I'm the Expert!

> **Learning Objectives:** To practice conversational Hebrew
> **Suitable for Hebrew Levels:** Intermediate
> **Playing Time:** 5-10 minutes
> **Materials/Resources Needed:** None
> **Variations:** Have students evaluate which of the expert's statements are true.

Helpful Hints: This is a good game to spark conversations.

How to play:
The teacher picks one student to be "An Expert."
Then, the teacher texts the student, via the chat box, a specific subject or profession to pretend to have expertise in.
The other students start asking the "Expert" questions in order to figure out this expertise. Once students find the correct answer, teachers should appoint another student to be the new "Expert" and assign a profession.
Expertise or professions may include bird watcher, dog sitter, professional sleeper, train pusher, etc.

Variations:
Once students uncover the profession of the "Expert," see if they can figure out which answers were true and which ones were false.

Game No. 81
What Happens Next

> **Learning Objectives:** Practice conversational Hebrew
> **Suitable for Hebrew Levels:** Intermediate
> **Playing Time:** 5-10 minutes
> **Materials/Resources Needed:** Video clips on YouTube or a sequence of images
> **Variations:** You can play the last scene of the clip or present the last image of the sequence and ask students to guess what happened before.

Helpful Hints: This game is easy to play.

How to play:

The teacher picks a random YouTube clip or a sequence of pictures. At a random point, the teacher pauses the clip and asks the students to guess what they think will happen next.

I'd suggest not picking a popular clip or a well-known story, and let students be creative with their ideas.

Variations:

The teacher may want to pause the clip at the last scene or the last image and ask the students to guess how they think it all started.

Game No. 82
But ... Why?

Learning Objectives: Practice question words in Hebrew
Suitable for Hebrew Levels: Intermediate
Playing Time: 5-10 minutes
Materials/Resources Needed: None
Variations: Specify the question word students must use.

Helpful Hints: This game encourages creative thinking skills, in addition to language acquisition.

How to play:
Teachers instruct the students that for the next three minutes they can ask anything they'd like to know about the teacher's hobbies. However, they must ask questions in Hebrew.
In return, the teacher will answer their questions, but only with a question in return.
For example, a dialogue may include something like the following:
"How many pets do you have?"
"I have three pets. How many dogs do you have?" etc.

Variations:
The teacher decides on one question word and instructs the students to ask any question, but they must use this specific question word in Hebrew. For example: "In the next minute, you may ask me anything you'd like, but you must use the question word: "כַּמָה"
Question words in Hebrew

QUESTION WORDS IN HEBREW — מִלּוֹת שְׁאֵלָה בְּעִבְרִית

Who	מִי
What	מָה
When	מָתַי
Where from	מֵאַיִן
Where to	לְאָן
Where	אֵיפֹה
Where	הֵיכָן
Why	לָמָּה
Why	מַדּוּעַ
How many	כַּמָּה
How	אֵיךְ
How	כֵּיצַד
Which	אֵיזֶה
Which	אֵיזוֹ
Which	אֵילוּ
If /whether	אִלּוּ
Will	הַאִם

Game No. 83
How do you Make ... ?

Learning Objectives: Practice conversational Hebrew
Suitable for Hebrew Levels: Intermediate
Playing Time: 5-10 minutes
Materials/Resources Needed: None
Variations: Students may record themselves demonstrating the activity in advance.

Helpful Hints: This game encourages student conversation. The teacher may want to collect presentation topics in advance.

How to play:
Prior to the lesson, ask students to send you an "expertise" that they possess.
Each student should have a few minutes to explain a favorite activity and teach classmates how to be experts.
For example, a student who likes cooking may wish to demonstrate how to make a favorite dish. A student who likes to play basketball may share favorite moves, etc.

Students should be instructed to demonstrate the activity, but also to use their Hebrew conversational skills to explain how and what needs to be done. It's highly recommended that students prepare, prior to their presentations, a list of related vocabulary words they'd like to use.
Some students may prefer to record themselves in advance and play the videos during the session.

Game No. 84
Are You Ready for Math?

> **Learning Objectives:** To practice counting numbers in Hebrew
> **Suitable for Hebrew Levels:** Intermediate
> **Playing Time:** 5-10 minutes
> **Materials/Resources Needed:** None
> **Variations:** Use basic counting for Hebrew beginners and more complex math questions for advanced students.

Helpful Hints: This game is a great review of numbers in Hebrew.

How to play:

The teacher writes the basic math signs on the screen:

וְעוֹד (+)

פָּחוֹת (-)

לְחַלֵק (:)

לִכְפֹּל (X)

הֵם (=)

The teacher asks each student to "challenge" another student in class with a math problem. Then, students, in their turn, present a math problem for another student to solve.

Teachers should make sure that the math problems are suitable for the class level.

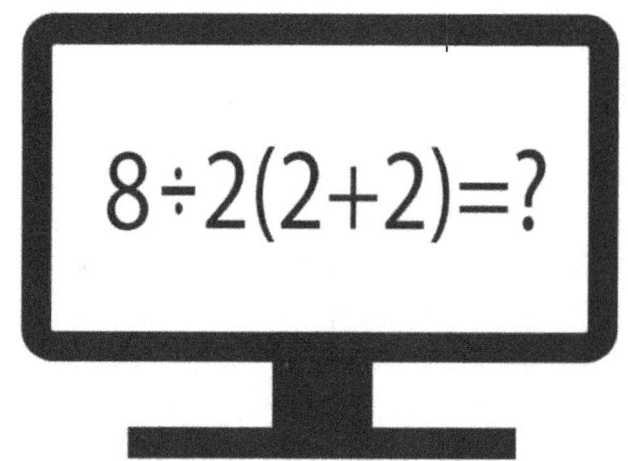

טַבְלַת הַמִּסְפָּרִים בְּזָכָר וּבִנְקֵבָה
NUMBERS COUNTING IN HEBREW M/F

	אחת	אחד
	שתיים	שניים
	שלוש	שלושה
	ארבע	ארבעה
	חמש	חמישה
	שש	שישה
	שבע	שבעה
	שמונה	שמונה
	תשע	תשעה
	עשר	עשרה
	אחת עשרה	אחד עשר
	שתים עשרה	שניים עשר
	שלוש עשרה	שלושה עשר
	ארבע עשרה	ארבעה עשר
	חמש עשרה	חמישה עשר
	שש עשרה	שישה עשר
	שבע עשרה	שבעה עשר
	שמונה עשרה	שמונה עשרה
	תשע עשרה	תשעה עשר

Game No. 85
Are You Ready for Math? Word Riddles

> **Learning Objectives:** Practice Mathematical Hebrew skills
> **Suitable for Hebrew Levels:** Intermediate
> **Playing Time:** 5-10 minutes
> **Materials/Resources Needed:** None / Teachers should prepare riddles in advance
> **Variations:** Use basic riddles for beginner students and more advanced ones for intermediate levels.

Helpful Hints: This is a fun review game. Make sure students know enough vocabulary words and numbers in Hebrew before playing this game, or challenge students to find the right answer.

How to play:
The teacher reads out loud or writes some math word problems.
The first student to solve the riddle must convince everyone else that there is more than one correct way to solve the riddle.
For example:

כִּתָּה אָלֶף יוֹצֵאת לַטִיוּל. בְּכִתָּה אָלֶף יֵשׁ 40 תַּלְמִידִים. בָּאוֹטוֹבּוּס יֵשׁ 56 כִּסְאוֹת.
כַּמָה כִּסְאוֹת רֵיקִים יֵשׁ בָּאוֹטוֹבּוּס?

Game No. 86
Are You Ready for Math? Gematria

Learning Objectives: A mathematical way to practice Hebrew.
Suitable for Hebrew Levels: Intermediate
Playing Time: 5-10 minutes
Materials/Resources Needed: None / Teachers should prepare riddles in advance
Variations: Divide the class into small breakout rooms. Each group should create a riddle to be solved by another group.

How to play:

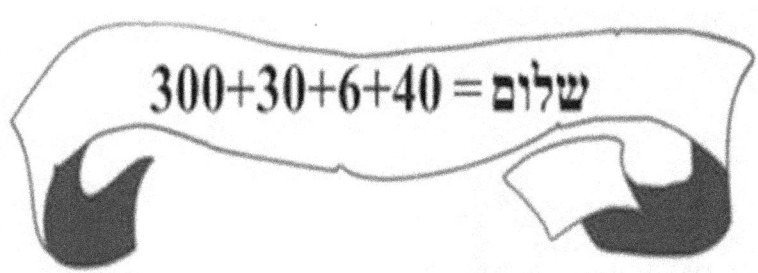

Points	Hebrew Letters	Points	Hebrew Letters
1	Aleph	30	Lamed
2	Bet	40	Mem
3	Gimel	50	Nun
4	Daled	60	Samekh
5	He	70	Ayin
6	Vav	80	Pe
7	Zayin	90	Tsadi
8	Heth	100	Qoph
9	Teth	200	Resh
10	Yod	300	Shin
11	Kaph	400	Tav

Gematria is a nice way of assigning numbers to the letters of the alphabet. In Gematria, each letter translates to a number.

There are a couple of ways to play games in Gematria. The teacher may write a phrase, sentence, or words on the screen and ask the students to translate it into numbers.

Another way to play is for the teacher to hide words or phrases behind the numbers and ask students to find what words are hiding there. For example, the number: 300+30+6+40 is equal to the word SHALOM שָׁלוֹם.

גִּימַטְרִיָה – מֵאוֹתִיּוֹת לְמִסְפָּרִים
GEMATRIA – FROM LETTERS TO NUMBERS

ל = 30	א = 1
מ = 40	ב = 2
נ = 50	ג = 3
ס = 60	ד = 4
ע = 70	ה = 5
פ = 80	ו = 6
צ = 90	ז = 7
ק = 100	ח = 8
ר = 200	ט = 9
ש = 300	י = 10
ת = 400	כ = 20

Game No. 87
Who is He and How Old is He Now?

Learning Objectives: A mathematical way to practice Hebrew
Suitable for Hebrew Levels: Intermediate to Advanced
Playing Time: 5-10 minutes
Materials/Resources Needed: Short bios of famous people
Variations: Teachers may assign the bios or ask students to come up with their own suggestions.

Helpful Hints: This game is aimed at advanced Hebrew levels who have learned the calendar years.

How to play:

The teacher pulls out short summary biographies of well-known people, including their birth and/or death dates, important bio information, profession, location and other facts that made them well-known.

The teacher does not mention the well-known person's name.

The students have five minutes to brainstorm (preferably in Hebrew) and try to guess the names of the famous people and their current ages (or, if they are dead, the age they would have been at the present moment in time).

For example:

זַמֶּרֶת יִשְׂרְאֵלִית מְפֻרְסֶמֶת, שַׂחְקָנִית וּמֻעֲמֶדֶת לִפְרָס גְּרָאמִי. נוֹלְדָה בִּשְׁנַת אֶלֶף תְּשַׁע מֵאוֹת חֲמִשִּׁים וְשֶׁבַע, וְנִפְטְרָה בִּשְׁנַת אַלְפַּיִם. הוֹרֶיהָ בָּאוּ לְיִשְׂרָאֵל מִתֵּימָן וְיֵשׁ לָהּ שִׁבְעָה אַחִים. בִּשְׁנַת אֶלֶף תְּשַׁע מֵאוֹת שְׁמוֹנִים וְשָׁלוֹשׁ הִיא שָׁרָה אֶת הַשִּׁיר הַמְפֻרְסָם "חַי"

(תְּשׁוּבָה: עָפְרָה חָזָה)

Game No. 88
Order in Court

> **Learning Objectives:** Practice conversational Hebrew
> **Suitable for Hebrew Levels:** Intermediate to Advanced
> **Playing Time:** 10 minutes
> **Materials/Resources Needed:** None /Teachers may want to prepare ethical questions in advance
> **Variations:** Teachers may want to assign roles or have students come up with their own roles.

Helpful Hints: This game should be timed, and each role should have no more than one to two minutes to present or argue. Keep the game dynamic and rolling.

How to play:
The teacher assigns roles (or lets the students assign their own), as if they are in court. Roles can be judge, prosecutor, witnesses, court clerk, jury, etc.
The teacher assigns a topic or a moral dilemma.
Let students take turns presenting their opinions. Let the jury decides who's winning the case.

Topics may be, for example: Sara used her **parents'** computer without their permission and found out unintentionally a secret that her parents kept from her. What should she do?

Students may come up with their own ethical dilemmas to be presented in court.

שקט בבית המשפט!

Game No. 89
Follow my Instructions

Learning Objectives: Practice listening comprehension in Hebrew

Suitable for Hebrew Levels: Intermediate to Advanced

Playing Time: 5-10 minutes

Materials/Resources Needed: None / Students may use white paper and a pen/pencil

Variations: Instead of using a command form, teachers may want to use Infinitives + בבקשה.

Helpful Hints: Fun and easy to play. This game is great to use as an evaluation of Hebrew skills during placement or at the beginning of the school year.

How to play:

The teacher reads out loud the following instructions.

Upon hearing the instruction students should act immediately.

Students who didn't hear or misunderstood the instruction should wait for the next assignment to be read out.

Here is the list of instructions in Hebrew (the teacher may add to the list or adjust according to students' Hebrew levels):

FOLLOW MY INSTRUCTIONS — עֲקֹוב אַחַר הַהוֹרָאוֹת

1)	צַיֵּר חֲמִשָּׁה עִגּוּלִים עַל הַדַּף
2)	קְפֹץ עַל רֶגֶל אַחַת שֵׁשׁ פְּעָמִים
3)	שִׂים אֶת הָעִפָּרוֹן עַל הָאֹזֶן
4)	הַקֵּף אֶת הַכִּסֵּא שֶׁלְּךָ שְׁמוֹנָה פְּעָמִים
5)	חֲשֹׁב עַל מִסְפָּר שֶׁקָּטָן מֵחָמֵשׁ וְגָדוֹל מֵאַחַת
6)	כְּתֹב שֵׁם שֶׁל חֵפֶץ יָרֹק
7)	שֵׁב עַל הָרִצְפָּה
8)	שִׂים שְׁתֵּי יָדַיִם עַל הָרֹאשׁ
9)	עֲנֵה בְּעַל־פֶּה: מִי הַיֶּלֶד הֲכִי גָּבוֹהַּ בַּכִּתָּה
10)	סְפֹר מִמִּסְפָּר 10 אָחוֹרָה עַד לְמִסְפָּר 1
11)	שְׁרֹק מַנְגִּינָה שֶׁאַתָּה אוֹהֵב
12)	הִתְבּוֹנֵן מֵהַחַלּוֹן וְסַפֵּר לִי מָה אַתָּה רוֹאֶה
13)	סַפֵּר לִי בְּדִיחָה
14)	קַח נְשִׁימָה עֲמֻקָּה
15)	חַיֵּךְ חִיּוּךְ רָחָב

Game No. 90
Book Party!

> **Learning Objectives:** To practice conversational Hebrew
> **Suitable for Hebrew Levels:** Intermediate to Advanced
> **Playing Time:** 10-15 minutes
> **Materials/Resources Needed:** None / Students should have their favorite books

Helpful Hints: This great game encourages conversations in Hebrew.

How to play:

The teacher presents a poll of five books from which students must select one they would like to read (even if they have never read it or heard about it before).

According to their answers, the teacher sends them into the breakout rooms.

Inside the breakout rooms, students have five minutes to answer the questions:

1. Why did they choose to read that book?
2. What other books were written by the same author?
3. If the author is currently working on his next book, what title should it have?

Conversations and new book titles should all be in Hebrew.

Game No. 91
Interview Me, Please

> **Learning Objectives:** To practice conversational Hebrew
> **Suitable for Hebrew Levels:** Intermediate to Advanced
> **Playing Time:** 5-10 minutes
> **Materials/Resources Needed:** None
> **Variations:** Real guests may be substituted by imaginary visitors, such as a pet or stuffed animal.

Helpful Hints: This fun game practices basic or complex conversational skills.

How to play:

There are two ways to play this game:

1. The teacher brings in a "guest" to sit in front of the video.
2. The students interview this individual by asking questions in Hebrew to learn more about the guest and the relationship with the teacher. For example, as a teacher, I may bring in my son, daughter, a neighbor or a friend. Students may ask guests about their families, where they live, their professions, etc.
3. The teacher may bring in a pet or a stuffed animal. Students need to ask "the special guest" questions, and the teacher answers on behalf of the "guest."

Game No. 92
My Hidden Secret

Learning Objectives: Practice conversational skills in Hebrew
Suitable for Hebrew Levels: Intermediate to Advanced
Playing Time: 5-10 minutes
Materials/Resources Needed: None

Helpful Hints: A fun game to practice conversational Hebrew.

How to play:
The teacher tells the students that there is a secret about to be shared with the group. The students, however, must ask the teacher questions in order to find out the secret.

The teacher may limit the number of questions, or answers to yes or no, or allow free conversations until the secret is revealed.

"Hidden secrets" can be: the number of pets I have at home, an interesting place I've visited, the number of siblings I have, etc.

סוד כמוס לפרה ולסוס

Game No. 93
Read My lips

Learning Objectives: Practice conversational skills in Hebrew
Suitable for Hebrew Levels: Intermediate
Playing Time: 5-10 minutes
Materials/Resources Needed: None

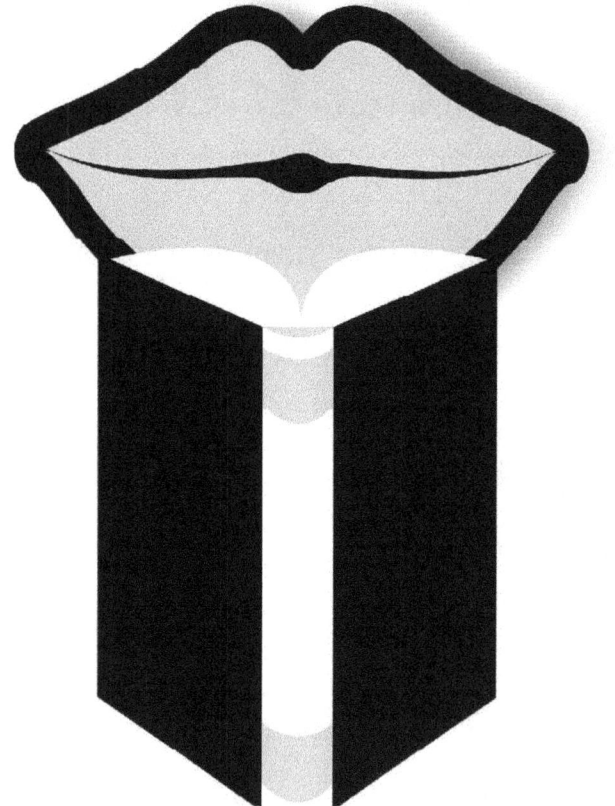

Read My Lips

Helpful Hints: This fun game helps students practice conversational Hebrew.

How to play:
The teacher texts via the chat box a phrase in Hebrew to a student volunteer.
The student says the phrase only by mouthing it without making a sound.
The other students need to guess the phrase.

Game No. 94
Where is He?

> **Learning Objectives:** To practice conversational skills in Hebrew
> **Suitable for Hebrew Levels:** Intermediate
> **Playing Time:** 5 minutes
> **Materials/Resources Needed:** None

Helpful Hints: This fun game provides conversational Hebrew practice.

How to play:
The teacher changes the background screen of one of the students with a place suggested on Zoom. The student whose background was changed can't see the new background, but everyone else can see it.
Students should not name the place, even if they know it, but should describe the place in Hebrew using their own words. For example: אַתָּה נִמְצָא בְּמָקוֹם שֶׁיֵּשׁ בּוֹ הַרְבֵּה בָּתִּים וּרְחוֹבוֹת קְטַנִּים
Or: אַתְּ נִמְצֵאת עַל הַר גָּבוֹהַּ עִם הַרְבֵּה דֶּשֶׁא וְעֵצִים
The student whose background was changed needs to guess the new location.

איפה אני???

Game No. 95
What Are You Selling?

> **Learning Objectives:** Practice reading and writing skills in Hebrew
> **Suitable for Hebrew Levels:** Intermediate
> **Playing Time:** 5-10 minutes
> **Materials/Resources Needed:** Students should have sticky notes

Helpful Hints: A fun game offers practice reading and writing in Hebrew.

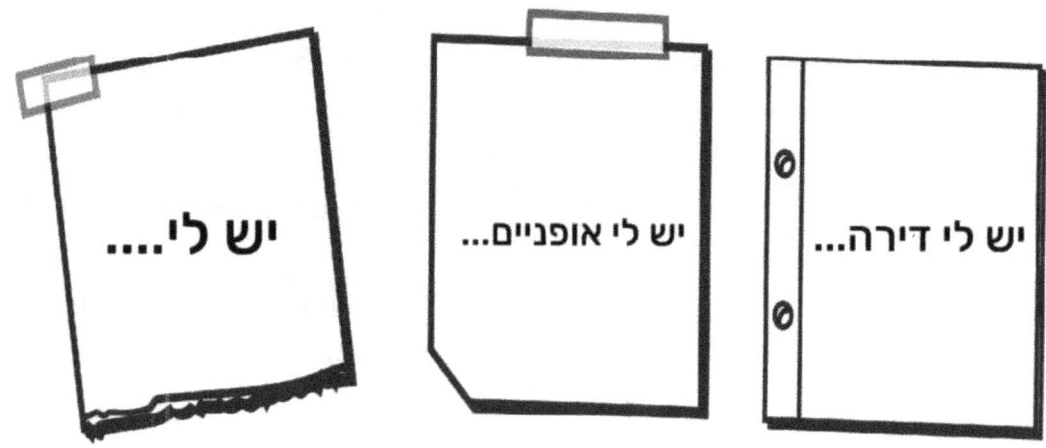

How to play:

The teacher instructs students to think about something they would like to sell.
Each student should have some sticky notes.
Upon an agreed sign, students have five minutes to write (in Hebrew) on the sticky notes some details about the product they are selling and why you should buy the product from them.

When finished, students should put the sticky notes on their faces or arms.
The other students read and figure out what each student is selling and why.
If they need clarification, they should ask the seller to explain.

Game No. 96
Why are You Late?

Learning Objectives: Practice conversational skills in Hebrew
Suitable for Hebrew Levels: Intermediate to Advanced
Playing Time: 5-10 minutes
Materials/Resources Needed: None

Helpful Hints: This fun game practices conversational Hebrew.

How to play:
The teacher or the group picks one student to "be at fault of being late again."
The student is sent to the virtual waiting room, while the group decides the reason behind the tardiness. The reason can be something silly or funny (e.g., he was late again because he had a long conversation with his plant).
Once the student is back from the waiting room, the other students provide hints about the reason for being late. The student "at fault of being late" needs to guess the reason that was chosen by the group.

Game No. 97
Domino of Words

> **Learning Objectives:** Practice vocabulary words in Hebrew
> **Suitable for Hebrew Levels:** Intermediate
> **Playing Time:** 5 minutes
> **Materials/Resources Needed:** None

Helpful Hints: A fun game gets the lesson started. Make sure to enable the annotation option. This game is similar to Scrabble.

How to play:

The teacher writes a word vertically and shares the screen. For example: יְרוּשָׁלַיִם

After the screen has been shared, each student uses the annotation option, either in handwriting or by entering a text box and adding words based on one letter of the given words. The letters in the given initial word can be used as the first letter of the new word, as the last letter or in the middle.

Keep filling in words until the screen is full or until time runs out. Here is an example:

				ד	ל	י					
						ר	ב	כ	ע		
			ן	ח	ל	ו	שׁ				
						שׁ	מ	שׁ			
	ד	ו	מ	ל	ל						
					ם	י					
						ם	י	ר	י	שׁ	

Game No. 98
What's for Dinner?

Learning Objectives: Practice conversational skills in Hebrew
Suitable for Hebrew Levels: Intermediate to Advanced
Playing Time: 5-10 minutes
Materials/Resources Needed: None

Helpful Hints: This is a fun game to start the lesson or end the class.

How to play:
Select four students to play this game. Two students act as the hosts, and two students are the tourists.

The Mystery Place

Explain the scenario: The tourists just came into town. They walk into a restaurant to try the local cuisine, and they have many questions as they want to learn about the local culture.

Upon an agreed signal by the teacher, they are "transported" into a new location and a new culture. The hosts are happy to help and answer any questions. The teacher, using the private chat box, sends the new location to the "hosts." Can students guess the tourist's new location?

For example: The tourists just walked into a small restaurant in an Israeli Shuk. Can they be "transported" into a small bakery in Paris?

Locations can be real or silly (e.g., a tent in the middle of an elephant farm or a coffee shop on the highest mountain).

Game No. 99
Make Flashcards Facts

> **Learning Objectives:** Practice writing and comprehension skills in Hebrew
> **Suitable for Hebrew Levels:** Intermediate
> **Playing Time:** 5-10 minutes
> **Materials/Resources Needed:** None

Helpful Hints: In advance of playing this fun game to get the lesson started, make sure to create an account on Quizlet.

How to play:
The teacher should create an account on Quizlet in advance. When it's time to play this game, the teacher shares the link in the chat box. Make sure to change the edit setting, so that all students can collaborate.

Each student writes down in Hebrew a hidden secret or a little-known fact about themselves on one side of the flashcard. On the other side, they write their names. Shuffle the flashcards and play the game.

Game No. 100
More Math in Hebrew

Learning Objectives: Practice mathematical concepts in Hebrew
Suitable for Hebrew Levels: Intermediate
Playing Time: 5 minutes
Materials/Resources Needed: None

Helpful Hints: This fun game practices mathematical skills in Hebrew.

How to play:
Each student randomly picks a two- or three-digit number that they keep secret.
Taking turns, each student tells everyone what to do with their numbers. For example, the first student says לִכְפֹּל בִּשְׁתַּיִם , and all students must use the number they choose and multiply by two. The next student says לְחַלֵּק בְּאַרְבַּע , and all students must divide their new sums by four.
At the end of the game, everyone must reveal the total number.
The student who has the lowest number wins.

תרגילי חשבון

Game No. 101
What's in the Dish?

Learning Objectives: Practice vocabulary words in Hebrew
Suitable for Hebrew Levels: Intermediate to Advanced
Playing Time: 5-10 minutes
Materials/Resources Needed: None.

Helpful Hints: This fun game works well at the end of class.

How to play:
The teacher presents an image of a tasty dish, like a cake, a fruit salad or an interesting soup.
The teacher then says: "How did I make it?"
The students then need to guess both the ingredients and the instructions for how the teacher made this yummy dish.
For example:
לִפְנֵי שֶׁמְּכִינִים סָלַט פֵּרוֹת צָרִיךְ לִשְׁטֹף הֵיטֵב אֶת הַתַּפּוּחִים, תּוּת הַשָּׂדֶה, הָעֲנָבִים, וּפֵרוֹת הַיַּעַר

מתכונים אליי בבקשה

Game No. 102
Lip-Sync Battles

Learning Objectives: Practice vocabulary words in Hebrew
Suitable for Hebrew Levels: Intermediate
Playing Time: 5-10 minutes
Materials/Resources Needed: None

Helpful Hints: This game is a fun way to get the lesson started.

How to play:
The teacher picks a popular and easy-to-follow song in Hebrew and places the lyrics on the screen.
Two students are chosen for the battle.
The teacher plays the song in the background, and the two students place competing videos on the screen. Make sure the students can read the lyrics.
The contestants should come up with a creative way to lip sync the words while making some gestures or dance moves. The contestants may also use props or costumes if they like.
The other students decide the winner of the lip-sync battle.

Addendum

נספחים -
שאלות חשיבה לפיתוח ועידוד השיחה בעברית

דִּילֶמָה מִסְפָּר 2

אַתָּה נוֹהֵג לַמִּשְׂרָד בַּיּוֹם חָשׁוּב מְאוֹד שֶׁבּוֹ עָלֶיךָ לְהַצִּיג אֶת הַפְּרוֹיֶקְט שֶׁלְּךָ בִּפְנֵי הַדִּירֶקְטוֹרְיוֹן. לְפֶתַע עֵץ נוֹפֵל וְחוֹסֵם אֶת הַכְּבִישׁ.
אַתָּה נִמְצָא בְּמֶרְחָק שֶׁל שְׁלוֹשָׁה מַיילִים, אֲבָל יֵשׁ לְךָ רַק 15 דַּקּוֹת עַד תְּחִלַּת הַפְּגִישָׁה.

מָה תַּעֲשֶׂה?

דִּילֶמָה מִסְפָּר 1

הַבּוֹס נָתַן לְךָ מִסְמָךְ חָשׁוּב מְאוֹד שֶׁיֵּשׁ לִמְסֹר לְבִנְיַן מִשְׂרָדִים אַחֵר, בְּמֶרְחָק קָצָר, תּוֹךְ 20 הַדַּקּוֹת הַבָּאוֹת.

זֶה יוֹם שֶׁמֶשׁ יָפֶה, וְאַתָּה מַחְלִיט לָלֶכֶת לְשָׁם בָּרֶגֶל. כְּבָר הִגַּעְתָּ לְאֶמְצַע הַדֶּרֶךְ כְּשֶׁמַּתְחִיל לָרֶדֶת גֶּשֶׁם חָזָק.

מָה תַּעֲשֶׂה?

דִּילֶמָה מִסְפָּר 4

אַתָּה הוֹלֵךְ בָּרְחוֹב וְדוֹרֵךְ בְּטָעוּת עַל מָה שֶׁנִּרְאֶה כְּמוֹ עֲרֵמַת חוֹל רְגִילָה. בָּרֶגַע שֶׁאַתָּה דּוֹרֵךְ בְּתוֹכָהּ, אַתָּה מֵבִין שֶׁהַחוֹל הוּא מֶלֶט רָטֹב וְרַגְלְךָ נִלְכְּדָה בְּתוֹכוֹ.
לְמַזָּלְךָ, אַתָּה מַחֲזִיק מַחְשֵׁב נַיָּד.

מָה תַּעֲשֶׂה?

דִּילֶמָה מִסְפָּר 3

סַנָּאִי מָצָא אֶת דַּרְכּוֹ דֶּרֶךְ דֶּלֶת הַכְּנִיסָה לַבַּיִת שֶׁלְּךָ. עַכְשָׁו, הַסַּנָּאִי בִּפְנִים וְלֹא יוֹדֵעַ אֵיךְ לָצֵאת. זֶה אַתָּה, הַסַּנָּאִי, וְהַכֶּלֶב שֶׁלְּךָ.

אַתָּה צָרִיךְ לְשַׁחְרֵר אֶת הַסַּנָּאִי מִיָּד לִפְנֵי שֶׁהוּא פּוֹגֵעַ בְּעַצְמוֹ אוֹ בְּמִישֶׁהוּ אַחֵר.

מָה תַּעֲשֶׂה?

דִילֶמָה מִסְפָּר 6

קִצַּרְתָּ אֶת שְׂעָרְךָ עִם מַכְשִׁיר תִּסְפֹּרֶת מְיֻחָד שֶׁנִּתַּן לְךָ עַל יְדֵי אָחִיךָ לִפְנֵי כַּמָּה שָׁנִים. כַּעֲבֹר כַּחֲצִי שָׁעָה אַתָּה מְגַלֶּה שֶׁחֲלָקִים מֵרֹאשְׁךָ כִּמְעַט קֵרְחִים וְאִלּוּ לַאֲחֵרִים יֵשׁ מַגָּע יָפֶה. נוֹסָף עַל כָּךְ, הַשָּׁעָה עַכְשָׁו חֲצוֹת וְהַמַּכְשִׁיר הַיָּשָׁן תָּקוּעַ וְלֹא יַעֲבֹד שׁוּב.

מָה תַּעֲשֶׂה?

דִילֶמָה מִסְפָּר 5

מַזָּל טוֹב! אַחֲרֵי שָׁבוּעוֹת שֶׁל עֲבוֹדָה כִּמְעַט וְהִשְׁלַמְתָּ פָּאזֶל שֶׁל 1,500 חֲלָקִים.

אַתָּה מֵבִין שֶׁכַּמָּה מֵהַחֲלָקִים הָאַחֲרוֹנִים חֲסֵרִים וְאֵינְךָ יָכוֹל לְהַשְׁלִים אֶת הַפָּאזֶל.

מָה תַּעֲשֶׂה?

דִילֶמָה מִסְפָּר 8

דּוֹדָתְךָ בִּקְשָׁה מִמְּךָ לִמְסֹר חֲבִילָה רְגִישָׁה לְאַחַת מֵחַבְרוֹתֶיהָ שֶׁגָּרָה בַּצַּד הַשֵּׁנִי שֶׁל הָעִיר. מָצָאתָ אֶת הַכְּתֹבֶת הַמְבֻקֶּשֶׁת וְחָנִיתָ לְיַד הַבַּיִת. כַּאֲשֶׁר אַתָּה מִתְקָרֵב, אַתָּה שׁוֹמֵעַ נְבִיחוֹת חֲזָקוֹת מֵאֲחוֹרֵי הַגָּדֵר וְרוֹאֶה כֶּלֶב עֲנָק מְחַכֶּה לְךָ בַּכְּנִיסָה.

מָה תַּעֲשֶׂה?

דִילֶמָה מִסְפָּר 7

אַתָּה חוֹזֵר הַבַּיְתָה בְּאֶמְצַע סוּפַת רְעָמִים וּמְגַלֶּה שֶׁאֶחָד הַחַלּוֹנוֹת בְּקוֹמַת הַקַּרְקַע פָּתוּחַ לִרְוָחָה וְתָקוּעַ. מֵאֻחָר מִדַּי לִקְרֹא לְמִישֶׁהוּ לָבוֹא, וְהָרוּחַ הָעַזָּה מַכְנִיסָה גֶּשֶׁם דֶּרֶךְ הַחַלּוֹן הַפָּתוּחַ.

מָה תַּעֲשֶׂה?

דִילֶמָה מִסְפָּר 9

חָנִיתָ אֶת מְכוֹנִיתְךָ לְיַד מַד חֲנָיָה צִבּוּרִי בָּרְחוֹב וְהִכְנַסְתָּ מַטְבְּעוֹת לְתַשְׁלוּם עֲבוּר שָׁעָה. כְּשֶׁאַתָּה חוֹזֵר לָרֶכֶב שֶׁלְּךָ כַּעֲבֹר 50 דַּקּוֹת, הַמַּד מַרְאֶה שֶׁהַזְּמַן עָבַר וְאַתָּה מוֹצֵא קְנָס עַל הַשִּׁמְשָׁה הַקִּדְמִית.

מָה תַּעֲשֶׂה?

דִילֶמָה מִסְפָּר 10

חֲבֵרְךָ לַעֲבוֹדָה מְאָרֵחַ מְסִבַּת תַּחְפּוֹשׂוֹת וְנִרְגָּשׁ לְהַזְמִין אוֹתְךָ. בָּרֶגַע הָאַחֲרוֹן אַתָּה מְגַלֶּה שֶׁנּוֹשֵׂא הַמְּסִבָּה הִשְׁתַּנָּה. בַּזְּמַן שֶׁכֻּלָּם לְבוּשִׁים כִּמְלָכִים, אַתָּה מוֹפִיעַ מְחֻפָּשׂ כְּמוֹ פָּרָה.

מָה תַּעֲשֶׂה?

דִילֶמָה מִסְפָּר 11

אַתָּה בַּדֶּרֶךְ לְאִמּוּן בַּחֲדַר הַכֹּשֶׁר. אַתָּה מַחֲנֶה אֶת הַמְּכוֹנִית בַּמִּגְרָשׁ הַקָּרוֹב בְּיוֹתֵר, אֲבָל מִבְּלִי לָשִׂים לֵב אַתָּה נִכְנָס לִשְׁלוּלִית מַיִם, וְעַכְשָׁו הַגַּרְבַּיִם שֶׁלְּךָ רְטֻבִּים. כַּמּוּבָן שֶׁאֵין לְךָ זוּג נוֹסָף אִתְּךָ.

מָה תַּעֲשֶׂה?

דִילֶמָה מִסְפָּר 12

אַתָּה נִמְצָא בַּבַּיִת וּמְחַכֶּה לְשִׂיחַת טֶלֶפוֹן חֲשׁוּבָה מְאוֹד מֵהַמִּשְׂרָד. בָּרֶגַע שֶׁאַתָּה נִכְנָס לַשֵּׁרוּתִים, גַּם הַטֶּלֶפוֹן הַבֵּיתִי וְגַם הַטֶּלֶפוֹן הַסֶּלוּלָרִי שֶׁלְּךָ מְצַלְצְלִים בּוֹ זְמַנִּית. הַטֶּלֶפוֹן הַבֵּיתִי נִמְצָא בַּמִּטְבָּח וְהַטֶּלֶפוֹן הַנַּיָּד נִמְצָא בַּמִּרְפֶּסֶת.

מָה תַּעֲשֶׂה?

דִילֶמָה מִסְפָּר 13

אַתָּה בַּמִּטְבָּח מְנַסֶּה מַתְכּוֹן חָדָשׁ לְעוּגִיּוֹת, אֲבָל אַתָּה לֹא יָכוֹל לִמְצֹא אֶת כּוֹס הַמְּדִידָה.

מָה תַּעֲשֶׂה?

דִילֶמָה מִסְפָּר 14

אַתָּה בֶּאֱמֶת חַיָּב לְהִשְׁתַּמֵּשׁ בַּשֵּׁרוּתִים הַצִּבּוּרִיִּים שֶׁבַּמִּסְעָדָה. יֶשְׁנָם שְׁלוֹשָׁה חַדְרֵי שֵׁרוּתִים, אַךְ שְׁנַיִם מֵהֶם תְּפוּסִים, וְהַמַּנְעוּל לַדֶּלֶת שֶׁבַּחֶדֶר הַשְּׁלִישִׁי שָׁבוּר, כָּךְ שֶׁהַדֶּלֶת לֹא נִסְגֶּרֶת.

מָה תַּעֲשֶׂה?

דִילֶמָה מִסְפָּר 15

אַתָּה רוֹכֵב עַל אוֹפַנַּיִם לַקַּנְיוֹן. בָּרֶגַע שֶׁהִגַּעְתָּ לְמִתְקַן חֲנִיַּת הָאוֹפַנַּיִם הַצִּבּוּרִי, אַתָּה מֵבִין שֶׁשָּׁכַחְתָּ אֶת הַמַּנְעוּל שֶׁלְּךָ בַּבַּיִת. אִם תַּשְׁאִיר אֶת הָאוֹפַנַּיִם לְלֹא נְעִילָה, יִתָּכֵן וְהֵם יֵעָלְמוּ. כַּמּוּבָן, אָסוּר לְהַכְנִיס אוֹפַנַּיִם אֶל תּוֹךְ הַקַּנְיוֹן.

מָה תַּעֲשֶׂה?

דִילֶמָה מִסְפָּר 16

הַכֶּלֶב שֶׁלְּךָ צָרִיךְ לָצֵאת הַחוּצָה, אֲבָל אַתָּה לֹא יָכוֹל לִמְצֹא אֶת הָרְצוּעָה שֶׁלּוֹ.
כְּבָר חִפַּשְׂתָּ וְלֹא מָצָאתָ אַף חֶבֶל בַּבַּיִת.
חֲנוּיּוֹת חַיּוֹת מַחְמָד כְּבָר סְגוּרוֹת הַלַּיְלָה.

מָה תַּעֲשֶׂה?

דִּילֵמָה מִסְפָּר 18

בִּזְבַּזְתָּ אֶת הַכֶּסֶף הַמְזֻמָּן הָאַחֲרוֹן שֶׁהָיָה לְךָ וְקָנִיתָ חֲבִילָה טְעִימָה שֶׁל אֱגוֹזֵי פִּיסְטוּק. אַתָּה מְגַלֶּה שֶׁרֻבָּם לֹא נִפְתָּחִים, לֹא מְשַׁנֶּה מָה תַּעֲשֶׂה.

מָה תַּעֲשֶׂה?

דִּילֵמָה מִסְפָּר 17

שְׁעַת אֲרוּחַת הַצָּהֳרַיִם הִגִּיעָה. אַתָּה רָעֵב. הַבֹּקֶר הָיִיתָ כֹּה עָסוּק וְדִלַּגְתָּ עַל אֲרוּחַת הַבֹּקֶר. זָכַרְתָּ לְהָבִיא אִתְּךָ לַמִּשְׂרָד סָלָט יְרָקוֹת וּפְרוּסַת קִישׁ. אַתָּה מְחַמֵּם אֶת הַקִּישׁ בְּמִיקְרוֹגַל וְאָז נִזְכָּר שֶׁשָּׁכַחְתָּ לְהָבִיא אִתְּךָ סַכִּין וּמַזְלֵג.

מָה תַּעֲשֶׂה?

דִּילֵמָה מִסְפָּר 20

טֶכְנָאֵי הַמַּחְשְׁבִים עָזַר לְךָ לְאַפֵּס אֶת הַסִּיסְמָה, וְעָלֶיךָ לִרְשֹׁם אוֹתָהּ בִּמְהִירוּת לִפְנֵי שֶׁתִּשָּׁכַח. הָעִפָּרוֹן הַיָּחִיד שֶׁמָּצָאתָ נִשְׁבַּר שׁוּב וָשׁוּב וּבְקָרוֹב לֹא יִשָּׁאֵר דָּבָר מֵהָעִפָּרוֹן ... אוֹ מֵהַסִּיסְמָה שֶׁלְּךָ.

מָה תַּעֲשֶׂה?

דִּילֵמָה מִסְפָּר 19

הַשִּׁיר מֵהָרַדְיוֹ נִתְקַע לְךָ בָּרֹאשׁ מֵאָז שְׁעוֹת הַבֹּקֶר, וְזֶה אֲפִלּוּ לֹא שִׁיר שֶׁאַתָּה אוֹהֵב. זֶה מְשַׁגֵּעַ אוֹתְךָ.

מָה תַּעֲשֶׂה?

Explore our additional books and resources
Available on Amazon.com

On Shapes and More
Roni Rosenthal | 2007

So, What do you know about being Jewish?
Roni Rosenthal | 2011

101 Let's Have Fun - 101 fun activities that reinforce learning in the Hebrew language
/ Roni Rosenthal | , 2009

Not by the Book: The Pencil Pro
Roni Rosenthal | 2018

Toolit - Open the box and let your ideas fly
Brand: The Pencil Pro

Visit our website: www.101Hebrew.com

www.ingramcontent.com/pod-product-compliance
Lightning Source LLC
Chambersburg PA
CBHW080443110426
42743CB00016B/3262